PLAN Cricket

PLAN Cricket

The Administrator's Bible

Christopher Bazalgette
& John Appleyard

THE POTWELL PRESS

Published by The Potwell Press
Purbrook Heath Road, Waterlooville, Hampshire PO7 5SA
C.D.E. Bazalgette & John Appleyard © 2003
ISBN 0 9546089 0 9
Typography by Iain Bain, Newnham, Herts SG7 5JX
Printed in Great Britain by the St Edmundsbury Press
Bury St Edmunds IP33 3TZ

The support of Kerr-McGee North Sea (UK) Ltd
is here gratefully acknowledged

By the same Authors
THINK-Cricket: Compete Mentally, 2001

'This book will give you an insight to understand that, by thinking the correct thought, you can improve your ability.'
ROBIN SMITH, former England batsman, Captain of Hampshire CCC.

'Describing the mental approach of successful captains, batsmen, bowlers, fielders and wicket-keepers. It gives you a wider dimension of the game. Read and discover the new performance levels obtainable.'
GORDON LORD, ECB Coach Education Manager.

'An excellent book, I thoroughly enjoyed it and it is a good insight for the young cricketer.'
TOM GRAVENEY, Gloucestershire and England.

'It is a neat little pocket book aimed at amateur cricketers who lack the resources of professional coaches. It stresses that there is much more to the game when your mind is fully focussed. It would suit school and club coaches.'
JOHN HOWELLS, Chief Coach
New Zealand Cricket, High Performance Centre.

COVER: President's Day at Warnford (Courtesy Hampshire Hogs CC).
FRONTISPIECE: Rolling out the Flicx artificial pitch.

Contents

Introduction

Cricket is a challenging sport played by men and women from all walks of life and of all ages. To take part at whatever level of competence is rewarding and should be fun.

However, before playing cricket it is necessary to Plan Cricket. This book provides a guide to running a successful cricket club. There are chapters on forming and running the committee, with details of each of the club officers' roles and the tasks that they will have to perform.

There are chapters on fund raising, social activities and club tours. The book stresses youth cricket and the value of encouraging youngsters to join the club. We highlight the plight of ex-players and remind them that as good club members they can still play a big part in running the club by training to be an umpire or scorer, and/ or learning the art of groundsmanship.

Each activity required to organise and operate a successful club is discussed and backed up with helpful data and contacts.

PLAN Cricket, which follows on from our previous book *THINK Cricket*, aims to streamline existing practices and stimulate members into contributing to a happy and well-run club.

It also includes a comprehensive section on companies and organisations that either provide services or supply products to cricket clubs.

Whilst every effort has been made by the authors to be accurate we cannot be held responsible for any product or service provided by a supplier.

Acknowledgements

PLAN Cricket has been the result of a 'need' that was learnt after working for *The Cricketer International* for thirty-two years. Every week we would receive a variety of questions, mainly from cricket club administrators, asking where they could purchase various equipment or services, or which organisation was responsible for this or that. Year by year questions remained similar to the year passed.

As authors we have had a great deal of experience in club cricket administration, which luckily has enabled us to cover organisational activites as well as the more practical areas, such as coaching and training. Probably our greatest combined strength has been to know to whom we should approach to find the modern techniques for those activities we learnt in the past.

Our first thanks should be to Gordon Lord and Hugh Morris at ECB Coach Education Unit for their direction and advice, duly followed by Ed Leverton who is responsible for setting up the Clubmark system. Similarly, David Winn, the Training and Development Education Officer for the Institute of Groundsmanship was a huge inspiration in providing the data required for cricket clubs and the route amateur groundsmen should take to improve their knowledge. We are indebted to the support we were given by Barrie Stuart-King, for his contributions for both the Club Cricket Conference and the Association of Cricket Umpires and Scorers, some of their developments will take time to come to fruition. However, this will enable our readers to have the opportunity to realise the thinking and planning that is taking place to further improve both organisations for the future.

We would like to thank Iain Wilton for his contributions on the work for MCC and Ian Stuart and Alison Davies on their activities at the European Office. We have endeavoured to provide all current and future club cricket administrators with an almanac of information on every activity they are likely to encounter in their running of a successful amateur cricket club. To achieve this it has been necessary to talk with a great many people and we thank them all for their input.

Special expertise was given by Peter Came on insurance for cricket clubs and cricketers; Barry Aitken on his work on Websites and keeping our writing properly focussed.

Our advertisers have provided details of their professional activities and we thank them for their support and encouragement.

We would like to acknowledge the kindness and support of Lyn Hilton, Donald Kenyon, Norman Davies, John Davison, Mandy Ripley, Peter Perchard, Lawrence and Ruth Green, Ian Reeve, Harry Constantine, Peter and Carol Cregeen and Mark Williams.

All authors must work long hours and therefore we thank our wives for their enduring support and great understanding.

Once a book has been written, it is nothing, unless there are people such as David Money, the successful author and cricketer, who expertly edited our work, and Iain Bain who was responsible for the typography.

Finally, we would like to thank enormously the man who has made it possible to publish PLAN Cricket, our dear friend Frank Sharratt, Chairman of Kerr-McGee North Sea (UK) Ltd.

C.B. & J.A.

1 Management Structure

This book provides all administrators and cricket club officers with a guide and structure on how to operate a cricket club. It covers the duties that each officer and the Executive Committee must carry out, and is designed to be an all-encompassing compendium of information.

The Roles of Club Officers and Committee

1 The President

The President's main responsibility is to ensure the club is run properly and lawfully. He presides over the Annual General Meeting.

The President directs the club to meet specific standards and will usually work unobtrusively with his committee to gain a professional result. In most clubs he is the figurehead, his role is usually to project the club image. He will probably head the financial committee, directing its professional course.

He will advise the Chairman on policy and will be the Club's representative at the highest level.

When influence is the requirement it will usually be the President who will be asked to act for the club.

In most clubs the committee elect the President.

2 The Chairman

The Chairman's responsibility is the whole structure of running the club. He is 'the hub' around which the committee and members revolve. He decides the club's role and how it will carry out that role. It is his responsibility to identify and gain officers to whom he can delegate the responsibilities of running the club. He is the man to set the targets for – committees, club officers and members. He sets out policy.

Specific factors that are his responsibility include discipline, communication and delegation, public relations, recruitment, training and development. He should supervise club management, efficiency and expertise. If the club has its own ground and head-quarters/pavilion, he will oversee the maintenance of buildings and ground, insurance and upkeep. He will also direct the club 'image', including club colours, their design and portrayal in clothing, stationery and flags.

He reports to the President, as everybody else reports to him.

He must be able to delegate his activities. Whilst setting goals he must check whether the goals are achieved and thank, encourage, and support his team.

3 The Club Secretary

He is the Chairman's 'right hand man'. he communicates the Chairman's instructions. He plans when meetings take place and where, he sets the agenda and distributes it. He must know the club's policy on every factor.

He takes minutes of all meetings and distributes them to committee members.

He will write all official letters on behalf of the club.

He will be the communication link with sub-committee chairmen, as well as their adviser on the matters that concern them, and should inform them and their committees about matters outside their jurisdiction.

He will keep the administration records of the club, and in most clubs will be the custodian of the club rules. He will be a man of total discretion.

4 The Treasurer

The Club Treasurer will be likely to have a financial background.

Most clubs in the country can unearth an accountant or, at worst, someone who is experienced with finances!

Maintaining good records of all income and expenditure within the Club is his vital role. He should receive regular reports from each sub-committee that earns or spends the Club's funds.

The Treasurer has to present audited accounts to the A.G.M each year and it is from these figures that a budget will be produced for the next 12 months. At the A.G.M he will be asked questions by the members and be expected to clearly explain the details of any entry on the accounts.

The Treasurer will advise the membership on annual subscriptions which, along with match fees, make up the largest guaranteed income of the year. If there is no Membership Secretary he will be responsible for collecting these subscriptions and, of course signing as many members on Direct Debit as possible, to make his job easier.

There is a need for a smoothly run system for the collection of match fees, as these funds should always reach him soon after every match has been concluded. Cash flow is the downfall of many clubs and small organisations. Further income to keep the club afloat is essential. The most obvious money earner is a bar in the pavilion which, when properly run, will yield considerable profit. The Treasurer must be a member of the management team that runs the bar. The Chairman of that sub-committee must report monthly to the Treasurer with a 'returns' sheet and a stock list that ensures that the monthly level of profit is maintained. In most clubs there will be volunteer members manning the bar. With amounts of cash about, as well as valuable stock, it is well that those who do help know that there is regular fiscal supervision and stock checks. A good idea is to have a written record of the names of those who work behind the bar and the dates of their duties.

Further club income can be obtained especially if the ground is in a good location by hiring part, or all, of the facility out to businesses for their annual cricket match. The pavilion can also be hired to local groups for daytime activities such as keep fit, bingo or coffee mornings.

Finally income can come from sponsorship. Advertising by local firms either in the annual fixture card or with display boards will help to increase the annual income. Perhaps a local business will offer a cup for a midweek competition; good publicity for them and more use of the club's facilities.

5　The Fixtures Secretary

This is a very important position. All the previous roles described have been dealing with the organisation of the internal running of the club, and this activity is for an organised individual. His role necessarily involves both the home club and their opposition, when and where matches are to be played, their duration, the organisation of match officials and ensuring everybody knows the location and venue and how to find the venue.

Normally it will be his responsibility to liaise with the groundsman and other club officials to set up each match.

He must be aware of the standard of the opponents and provide a balanced team. He provides a report to the Annual General Meeting on the results of the past season and the planned fixtures for the next season.

He needs to keep a good 'contacts' list of other clubs fixtures secretaries, knowing their names, addresses, telephone numbers at work and at home, an e-mail address if there is one, so he can always make contact should an emergency occur. It is useful, once a fixture list has been created, to advise each team captain of the opposition's fixtures secretary's name and their captain, and to provide contact details.

Clubs must provide the finalised match list for printing fixture cards well before the season starts, so all club members can plan their availability. As most clubs play in leagues the Fixtures Secretary must be in contact with the league organiser as well. His efficiency will effect the club's image, so it is vital he keeps proper records.

6 The Membership Secretary

This is another extremely responsible activity, for he should keep the names and addresses and contact information with all players who are members of the club. It will be useful if the players' strengths are recorded as well: i.e. where they normally bat, which type of bowler, whether they are left or right handed, if a wicket-keeper, or if they are prepared to act in an umpiring role. The membership secretary will also keep records regarding new members – who proposed and seconded them, who might be playing 'qualifying' matches, and when they come 'up' for election.

Other activities will include printing membership proposal forms; all administration regarding club members and club officials; dealing with resignations, and recording members who die or retire. In some clubs he may be responsible for chasing up slow or non-payers of subscriptions!

7 The Grounds Director

This person will have full knowledge of all the club's grounds, their plans for the next two or three seasons. He must know all the requirements for purchasing machinery, materials and equipment and the functions that will be carried out in maintaining all the ground facilities.

This will usually include scoreboards/boxes or fascias, boundary markers, sight screens, artificial pitches, pitch covers and practice nets, boundary nets and car parking. He will also plan the preparation of each pitch, the square, the outfield and their repair before and after the season, and maintenance during the season.

The Director will deal with the groundsman, his training, his management and employment. He will report to the Executive Committee and the Annual General Meeting. He will attend the Finance Committee meetings, supplying the groundsmanship costings for the season to come and providing an explanation of what has been spent.

8 The Groundsman

This person has the responsibility to prepare each ground for each match and all the matches throughout the season. This is one of the most crucial activities for the success of the club and will affect the quality of members' and performances, how they play. It will also reflect the image of the club and its standing with the opposition.

The Groundsman has to plan to 'consolidate' his square before the season.

He then must plan how many pitches he can use on the square and which are the most important matches, ensuring that the pitches are played upon in the correct order. He is responsible for his equipment, its maintenance and its repair.

Besides looking after his working equipment, he must maintain all the ground accessories. sight screens, scoreboards ,pitch covers, etc.

He has to know when to mow, when to roll, when to use fertiliser and when to water. He must know about drainage and irrigation and take care of all surrounds to the cricket ground. He has to know how to obtain bounce and pace from his pitch. This will mean working long hours in all weathers and 'tending his ground' with care. He reports to the Grounds Director.

9 The Bar/Catering Manager

This is one of the most important activities within any sports club, for this operation is where large profits can be made. If the club has a 'brewery' trained manager it is a huge advantage. He should know the place to buy, at what cost and the price to sell; he can prepare the 'cellar', be able to clean the pipes, reduce spillage to a minimum and change barrels. He will know the 'life' of beer barrels and lager and other popular brands to stock.

Regulating the demand is vital to the profitability of each bar plus, which means making regular stock takes. Running an efficient bar means having enough personnel working on a rota basis. Some clubs have a team of Bar Stewards responsible for specific matches. Unless there is no alternative, it is advisable that players do not 'run' the bar for the match in which they are playing. At times they may not necessarily have cash in their playing apparel, or just forget to repay their bill. If this only happens once per match, the loss soon mounts up.

10 The Fund-raising Secretary

This activity is more likely to be set up as a sub-committee, but somebody has to lead the operation and so is included. There are always periods when the club requires extra funds, over above what is budgeted for on an annual basis.

The person in question requires an outgoing personality – someone who can gain the help of fellow members and 'persuade' the business fraternity to sponsor his club, both in large activities and smaller ones. In many cases he will be a businessman with 'selling' training. The Fund-raiser must clearly have a reason for raising the money and so must prepare a plan, budget and keep records. Currently it helps if he is computer literate and a good communicator, as he has to advise others about the project, and keep the club and club officers aware of his progress. It is vital he gains the confidence and support of his fellow club members.

He must be a good delegator, and though he is directing the activity, it is important that he obtains others to do much of the work. If he becomes 'bogged' down working at the little chores, he will not be able to see the full picture and thus minimise the overall success of the project.

11   The Entertainments Secretary

Like the Fund-raiser most of his activities require a similar 'flair'. These may involve distinct operations for club members, members' friends and arranging bookings of the club's facilities by outside agencies. Events that come under his banner would be 'Club Dinners', 'The Club Ball', 'Presentation Evenings', 'Barbecues' and 'The Club Picnic'. His main activity is to be a good organiser. He is the man who could easily act as the 'M.C.' for any event, or run a club auction or organise a disco, or openly 'beg' for raffle prizes.

12   The Club Publicity Officer

Few clubs have a publicity officer, though in this age of sponsorship a good one will help to create sponsors, as well as keep them. He will be able to 'steer' the image set by the Chairman. He should arrange for all matches to be reported, giving recognition to the various teams and their personnel. When playing sport, especially team games, it is vital club members have loyalty to the club and are proud of their club. The Publicity Officer will have a pivotal role in establishing both these points, as well as maintaining them. Similar to other officers he will work closely with the Club officers and team captains. He will work closely with The Chairman and General Club Secretary on the image of the club, club colours, and club flag, leisurewear and training wear. He will aim to have excellent contacts with the local press, television and radio personnel, plus specialist press. His responsibility will be two directional: firstly, he will create a style for the club's promotional articles, and secondly, he will find out what type of material the media require.

He will naturally help the Entertainments Secretary and the Fund-raising Secretary, as publicity is required both in the club and for the general public. Publicity is not just the writing of press releases or writing match reports, it might be attending other club

*(The use of pronouns indicating the male gender is purely for brevity).

dinners or league functions; thus developing the club image by ensuring the club is always represented. He will need to 'watch over' all material emanating from club officers.

13 The Equipment Manager

This person is responsible for the 'club' equipment available for the cricket team, looking after repairs and maintenance, and ensuring that the kit is always returned from an away fixture, or properly put away after the home match. He should ensure that when the gear wears out it is suitably replaced.

He should purchase a wooden mallet for knocking in bats, a 'cone' for putting rubber grips on to bat handles, make sure all the stumps and bails are in good condition and have spares of bails, as well as 'heavy' bails for when it is very windy. He should have bat oil, keep umpires coats clean and have them laundered before the season.

He needs to keep a check on wicket-keeping gloves for repair and whether they meet the new law requirements. Either at the end of the season or before the next season he should check on the new cricket balls needed to ensure they are ordered in time for delivery before the season.

14 The Club Historian

Few clubs think of having a record of their development from the first day. It is the Founder's task to look for a responsible person likely to be methodical and tidy and think in a procedural pattern. Obviously finding a member who has a passion for such activities will be a great advantage. He will need the knack of spotting and recording the current events and memorabilia that will be of most interest in the future. At the beginning, the keeper of club records will be photographing the development of the ground and the pavilion; he must also remember to include people in his photographs preferably in typical poses that relate to their contribution to the club's progress. It is vital to also record documents such as planning applications, bar licence, local newspaper reports, and club members' activities that might be peripheral to the main activity. As the club gets bigger there will be more material, he will need storage space as time goes on. It is probable that buildings will be extended and better practicing facilities constructed. There are many occasions when one visits a cricket club and are told about the original thatched pavilion and there is no record anywhere to enhance the story. Remember that the ground equipment that you buy today will be ancient in years to come, so photograph these items in operation. All this written material can, of course be kept on computer and recovered, whenever required in the future.

Photographs, printed matter, brochures of special club activities and all club books should be kept in dry storage when not on display in the clubhouse. Members playing achievements must be saved and highlighted by written and photographed records, particularly relevant when a player (whether junior or adult) achieves higher honours such as being selected to represent the County team.

All paintings and framed artifacts should be photographed as proof of value and record, in case of theft or fire (the photographs kept separately to where the items are stored). The collection will soon become valuable in an historical sense and should be valued for insurance at regular intervals.

If the records can be indexed, even better, so members can extract information at a later date. Details of sources should be kept, so if and when items are reprinted, the correct authority can easily be sought and gained.

The older the club, then all records become the more interesting – keep your local paper informed about memorable dates and arrange a two-way flow of information. Should the ground or buildings change, then all should be recorded for posterity. Do not forget achievements gained by club officers and members, who might be or have been officers of the County Club when they held office and the accomplishments of prominent players who have died. Records of such members who gained national or international selection are obviously of prime interest.

15 'Tea Arranger'

In many amateur clubs match teas are the responsibility of the Team Captain, who will probably delegate team members to help with this task. However, in many cases it will be a wife or girlfriend who will do most of the work. Some clubs have a rota system of supporters who carry out the task.

The Club will designate how much should be spent, in terms of a maximum, on ingredients and provision of sandwiches and cakes, milk, tea and sugar. It is also normal for the Home team to provide this meal for each side, umpires and scorers. After the meal it is necessary to clear up and wash up the crockery, if the home team is batting then those not actually at the crease may help wash up, it is unfair to expect 'the Preparer' to do this job week-by-week.

If you have supporters they will expect a cup of tea and a sandwich, for which you can charge. There will be a charge for both teams, but not for umpires and scorers.

If the 'Tea arranger' is not necessarily an actual member of the club, their activity must be covered by insurance – this is the employer's insurance. They must have proper worktops so they can prepare the food cleanly and safely and there must be a separate wash basin or sink so they can wash their hands. (Health & Safety) regulations.

Lunches, Dinners and Special Events

For clubs who play all-day matches or require lunches and dinners, it is more likely that they will have a company on a long-term contract to provide the food. If this is the case there should be a cooker, washing-up machine and refrigerator available. There should be a number of cupboards, as well as worktops on which to prepare the food. If you look after your staff, they will respect the club much more and you will find the results far more pleasing.

If you have someone to cook barbecues after special matches, detail team members to help lay up tables, take the money and, most important, clear up afterwards, including washing-up.

Remember to provide a float, unless the barbecue organiser does this for himself/herself.

If possible always have a table-cloth - presentation is important, it tells your opponents that your club cares and they will react favourably.

Food

If those who are preparing the food are amateurs, it is a good idea to put up a notice asking all those preparing food to wash their hands beforehand.

With more people of different nationalities playing the game, it is a good idea to have an alternative meal, in case of emergency. There can also be a problem with so many allergies these days, so plan ahead. Where possible nuts should be avoided, or people advised when nuts are included.

If you have spectators supporting the club consider supplying tea, soft drinks and possibly ices, by the end of the season all your profits mount up.

Management Tree

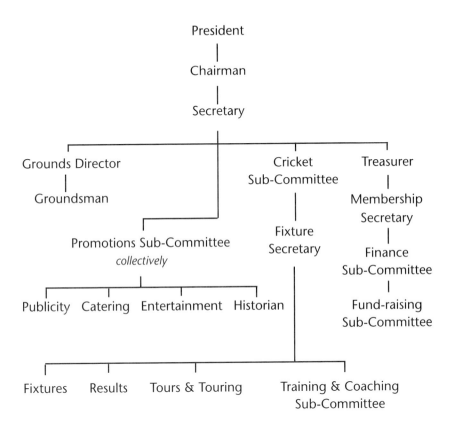

2 Administration

The Law · Insurance · Grants and Applications for Funding
Club Constitution · Membership · Fundraising · Relocation of
a Cricket Club · The Values of a Website

1 The Law

Every club needs to set up its club rules. Accounts must be kept
and the Club must have an Annual General Meeting to approve
the accounts every year,

If the club has licensed premises, then a licence must be gained
from the local Magistrates' Court annually (*see* p.147)

If the club has buildings on its ground then the Council Tax
must be paid, as must the water rates and the payment for electricity consumed.

Each Club should keep records of the property, either owned or
leased/rented, so it is aware of any 'Rights of Way' others may have
over the land. Other requirements may include the maintenance
of pipes and drainage, fencing and the reaction neighbours may
have if cricket balls damage their property. There is no defence in
saying the cricket ground was there before the houses were built.

If a Club officer or member has any doubt regarding the Law's
requirements, official advice should be obtained as quickly as possible.

However, if any disagreement should occur it is best to sort it out
before 'going to law'.

2 Insurance

Insurance is now a very important factor, as without both the
correct cover for the individual and the club itself. One claim can
financially cripple the club and its officers. Sadly, solicitors and

others now believe there are no accidents, there is always someone to blame.

Every club, with or without its own premises, must have 'Public Liability' insurance. This will cover all club members for accidents whether they are damaged on their home ground or at away matches. In order to cover paid personnel, such as ground staff, umpires and scorers, it is advisable to take out an employers' insurance policy.

People acting as helpers, be they wives or girlfriends, providing catering support or temporary bar staff, should be made honorary members for the day.

Similarly, guest players will also receive the same honorary status. However, there should be a statement to that effect in your club rules/policy, otherwise the insurer might refuse to pay out. Not all clubs have a personal playing insurance policy for their members, individuals are advised to have their own personal accident scheme. Clubs can buy units of cover to pay for accidental injury such as dentistry, optical and temporary disablement as well as death and total disablement.

All buildings should have adequate cover against damage, for whatever reason, including pavilions, scoreboxes, machinery storage buildings or outside lavatories.

There should be insurance for all machinery and materials.

Whoever is responsible for these areas, together with sight screens, pitch covers and artificial pitches, should be aware of their true value. It is vital for club finances that all items are regularly inspected, a record kept of the inspection date and each item is properly maintained.

The other factor affecting club's insurance is Security.

Unless a retainer is permanently residing on the premises, then the security of the cricket pavilion is a major problem.

Usually the cricket club's location is remote, which means the pavilion is an easy option for a burglar. Most clubs aim to leave no valuables on-site when it is not being used. However, the thief does not know this and can do a lot of damage even though nothing valuable has been taken.

By choice, security should be considered and put in place when the pavilion is built. The use of bars for windows, extra-strong glass and special locks being put into the manufacturing process.

Probably the most sought-after theft is the lawn mower, many being taken weekly. Therefore it is vital that any store where the machinery is stored is as burglar proofed as possible. In some cases heavy padlocks can be used. It might be possible to prevent a vehicle being used to carry the stolen equipment, by denying access to the ground. Some clubs consider the use of video cameras and others have direct links to the police station. The more complicated the security, the more costly it becomes. What clubs must do is provide a balance between the overall cost and what the club stands to lose. Obviously the more break-ins that are made, the greater becomes your insurance charges. Again the best way to sort this problem is talk with your insurance broker and/or your police Crime Prevention officer.

Most clubs have a policy arranged with their cricket league, who have negotiated a group deal for all the clubs in the league. The group rate is preferential to the singular route.

There is an ECB 'Extra Cover' Insurance Scheme operated by Marshall Wooldridge (Tel: 0800 289301). They have pointed out that only members benefit from this policy unless prior arrangements are made.

This is an example of what is available through a group league scheme:

The Hampshire Cricket League Insurance Scheme. This is a very comprehensive policy that provides all the relevant covers that would be required by a cricket club.

As various insurance companies are named, this does not mean they are the only companies with such a policy, but it gives the reader a basis for the areas he/she requires to cover.

Special extension to Public Liability: Irrespective of liability the General Accident will agree to pay up to £250 to cover third party vehicle damage caused by stray cricket balls, which is not provided for under the third party's own Private Car comprehensive policy.

This extension, will not apply to any person who has third party or third party fire and theft insurance only cover, nor will it apply to Club members, players both insured and visitors and other people attending the cricket match or function are excluded.

N.B. *In the event of a possible claim being made under this section liability must not be admitted by the club or its members.*

SECTION 3

ALL RISKS INSURANCE

Only available if Personal Accident cover is operative.

Schedule A

Club equipment (loss or damage anywhere in the United Kingdom) Club cricket bag and contents – if playing away games with the club equipment.

Club Trophies (Please supply inventory of trophies if sum insured exceeds £1600.) A minimum sum insured of £1000 applies.

Exclusion

This excludes breakages in play, member's own items, theft from unlocked vehicles and items not usually associated with a cricket bag contents.

Schedule B
Additional playing equipment

Non turf pitches.
Netting and poles
Pitch covers and sight screens; scoreboards, boxes and fascias.
NOTE: Sight screens left in the open out of season will not be covered unless they are made secure with padlock and chains.
A minimum sum insured of £1000 applies.

Exclusions

1.   Cover will not apply to netting and supporting poles out of season unless they are stored or used inside a secure building.

2.   The first £25 of each and every claim.

Schedule C
Groundsmen's equipment

Mowers

Rollers

Spikers

Tractors, and other motorised vehicles (up to a maximum sum insured of £1500. Tractors and vehicles above this value will be considered upon application). Implements. Tools. Fertilisers etc.

A minimum sum insured of £1000 applies.

Exclusions

1.   Theft other than by forcible and violent entry or exit from any building or vehicle.

2.   Accidental damage whilst in use.

Extension of Cover

Tractors and motorised items of Groundsmens' machinery will be covered whilst in the open providing and subject to the ignition keys being removed and/ or the item of machinery being immobilised whilst not in operation.

This extension of cover is subject to the insured paying £250 of each and every claim.

In their own interest clubs should ensure machinery and equipment are stored in a locked secure building.

SECTION 4

PROPERTY DAMAGE

only available when section 1 Personal Accident and section 2 Liability are operative.

Cover available for Club houses, Pavilions, Stores and contents (providing cover against Fire, Aircraft, Explosion, Impact, Earthquake, Riot, Civil commotion or Malicious Damage, Storm, Tempest and Flood and Theft by forcible or violent entry or exit to and from buildings)

PLAN Cricket

Exclusions

1. The first £50 of each and every claim in respect of Malicious and water damage

2. The first £50 of each and every claim in respect of Theft involving forcible and violent entry or exit.

3. Buildings of standard construction are deemed to be built of brick, stone, concrete, metal or asbestos and roofed with slates, tiles, concrete, metal asbestos or felt.

The following sections are only available if Contents are insured under SECTION 4 – Property Damage.

SECTION 5

MONEY in GAMING MACHINES

Theft of money from gaming machines – sum insured £250.

SECTION 6

BUSINESS INTERRUPTION

(This section is relevant especially for clubs. So in the event of a disaster, i.e. fire or storm – replacement facilities can be temporarily provided until a new pavilion etc can be put in place this protects the income of the club).

Loss of income arising from fire, aircraft, explosion, impact, earthquake, riot, civil commotion or malicious damage, storm, tempest and flood, and theft by forcible or violent entry – sum insured £25000.

SECTION 7

LOSS of LICENCE

(only works if the local council change their licencing laws and not because of loss of licence due to police involvement)

Loss sustained by the Insured as a result of the licence for the sale of excisable liquors being

a) Forfeited under the provisions of the regulations relating to such licence

b) Refused renewal by the licencing authority.

Provided that each forfeiture or refused renewal results from causes beyond the control of the Insured.

The amount payable shall be the depreciation in value of the interest of the insured in the premises or the business caused by such forfeiture or refused renewal but not exceeding the Limit of Liability of £50,000 and costs and expenses incurred by the Insured with the written consent of the Insurer in connection with any appeal against such forfeiture or refused renewal.

SECTION 8

LOSS of FOOD in DEEP FREEZER

The deterioration of food as a result of accidental power loss or breakdown of machinery.

This insurance will pay for the replacement of food up to a maximum limit of £500.

Exclusions

Deliberate act of switching off the freezer.

10% or £25 whichever is the greater is excluded from every claim where the refrigerating unit is more than 5 years old.

SECTION 9

Money

Automatically included if Section 3 All Risks or Section 4 Property Damage are operative.

Money Insurance (the property of the Cricket Club)	
Money in Transit	£1000
Money in Club premises during occupancy	£1000
Money in homes of club officials	£250
Money in club premises during unoccupancy or overnight	£25

No Claims Discount

All clubs that insured under our scheme during the last two years will be offered a No Claims Discount.

The scale will be:

31

| 1 year claim free | 10% |
| 2 consecutive years claim free | 15% |

New clubs joining the scheme will be entitled to a maximum of 10% providing they can provide written proof of no claims. The Secretary and Chairman must jointly sign a letter to say there have been no claims during the last year of insurance nor are there any outstanding or unreported claims or incidents which might give rise to a claim.

Claims Procedure

All claims should be reported immediately in the first instance to: J.Caldwell of Paul Jones Insurance Services Ltd., Kings House, 316 Shirley Road, Southampton SO15 3HL. Telephone No. 02380 788444

Claims must be notified that within 20 days of the incident, failure to do so may invalidate the claim.

This is only a summary of the insurance cover and full details of the policy terms and conditions can be found in the master policy, a copy of which is available from Paul Jones Insurance Services Ltd.

3 Grants and Applications for Funding

Most clubs, at some time in their period of growth, require to raise large amounts of money. In this chapter we provide guidelines on how a club should tackle this particular problem.

Putting your application together

Every grant application should show that your club has created funds through determined efforts of fundraising (*see* Chapter 1, p.17).

Careful planning to ensure your ambitions are realistic and right for your club is critical. Extra advice can be gained from the ECB booklet (Model Development Plan) that provides a format and procedure, approved by the main Grant Aid providers, to help you do this.

Your plan forms a statement of your future intentions and will demonstrate to funding agencies how your plans will satisfy their requirements adding to the cricket provision in your area.

It is also important at this stage to identify a timescale outlining when you intend to implement each element of your plans.

Before starting your planned operation contact your County Development Officer at the County Cricket's Main office. Tell him of your plans and ask him for his advice. (*see* Note 1, p.119)

Costing your plan

Once you have assessed what you currently have and decided upon your chosen future direction, it is vital you then put some detailed costing to your plans. These can be in the form of quotations from contractors and/or suppliers or costs in 'man hours'.

This will help you assess what financial support you will need and allow you to chart your best possible route to obtain the funds your proposed developments require.

Approaching the relevant Fund Organisations

It is important that you choose the correct funding agency(s) for your respective plan/elements within your plan.

Each organisation has its own particular criteria and requirements. It is therefore vital that you make contact with the individual organisation and match your plans to its respective criteria before you compile an application.

Pre-planning

It is very important to show how your plans will help your community.

Thus you must be able to indicate what access the community has, either as direct access to your new facility, or through an ability to join your club. If possible this should include minority groups, such as the disabled, women, and young people. It is most important to encourage youth, if you do not have a youth section, you should start one (*see* Chapter 3). Include the provision of quality coaching and supervised activity of juniors.

Work out the leisure facilities around the location of your club, include numbers of population and any plans that might be in the offing for increasing the number of new houses being built. Consider transport availability – especially public transport. But do your research properly, the better your plan the greater is your chance that your request will be accepted.

Tips for Achieving a Successful Application

a. *Prepare your application*

¶ Make sure your plans are thorough, have been costed and have an identified timescale.

¶ Ensure you have, and can identify, the people and resources available to run the project after it has been built, installed or set up.

¶ Where relevant, demonstrate how your plans have strategic relevance – refer to the County, Regional and/or National Cricket/Sport Development Plans.

¶ Consult as widely as possible before submitting your application(s).

¶ Ensure the timescale of your plans is in line with that of the funding agency(s).

¶ Plan your cash flow thoroughly, as some funding agencies will only release funds on completion of works.

¶ Ensure, where necessary, you have the relevant planning permission or written confirmation that it is not required.

¶ Any equipment purchases or facilities you install should meet certain design and/or performance criteria. For guidance please refer to relevant Sport England Guidance Notes and ECB technical specifications (contact your CDO for details).

¶ Utilise all the help that is available from the ECB, the respective funding agency, consultants and Sport England.

b. *Cost your plan*

¶ You should demonstrate how your project represents value for money.

¶ Emphasise your level of need for financial support (based on your annual accounts).

¶ Make sure your application is honest and you request only funds you require.

¶ Be prepared to undergo a process of monitoring by funding agencies. Some agencies reserve the right to reclaim funding if they are not satisfied with its use.

¶ Have contingency plans in the event of a rejected application or a reduced award.

c. *Approach the Relevant Funding Organisations*

¶ Your application must demonstrate clear plans in accordance with the criteria or the respective funding agency.

¶ Where necessary forward any consultation forms as required by the funding agency.

¶ Submit your application ahead of deadlines set by respective funding agencies.

¶ Apply to the number of funding organisations you need to ensure the funding you require.

¶ Identify, where necessary in your application(s) other sources of partnership funding.

¶ Include details of other confirmed awards and, where not confirmed when you expect to receive a decision.

¶ Check how much you are eligible for. Some funding agencies make provision in certain urban and rural areas for additional support.

¶ Ensure your chosen funding organisations are complementary. Some agencies will not commit to funding if certain others have been applied to.

¶ Ensure the tenure of your ground is of sufficient length as set by the respective funding agency. Most funding agencies require a minimum of ten years lease, freehold, or other security of tenure.

¶ DO NOT START ANY PROJECTS or PLANS before you receive official written notice of award or permission to go ahead. Most funding agencies will not fund retrospectively.

¶ Consider every possible option available including sponsorship, Sportsmatch, donations, loans, fund raising activities etc.

¶ You should give the funding agency full recognition for any support – letters of thanks, plaques, local publicity etc., should be considered to recognise their generosity.

Armed with this information every club should now be in the position to submit a strong application for funding. There are many organisations, which have money available. Your CDO is a vital source of information.

* Note: This information was supplied from the publication *Developing Your Club*, 'Sources of Grant Aid and Cricket Funding', compiled by F.M.Turner MBE, ECB Consultant. The Editors are indebted to him and the ECB for the help and support they have provided and for allowing them to reproduce this information.

FUNDING AGENCIES

Sport England Lottery Fund – including the Community Projects Fund, the latter is the most relevant to cricket. For this fund there are a number of key target groups: Areas of socio-economic deprivation, Young people, Ethnic minorities, people with disabilities, women and girls.

Awards for All projects requiring a grant between £500 – £5000.

Preferred Projects for Cricket This includes Pitch Preparation with emphasis on new or upgraded equipment for junior clubs, or clubs with junior sections, and/or special advice, materials and training in groundsmanship. All training & Education that includes Course fee payment/subsidy, e.g. National Coaching Scheme, ECB/IOG Groundsmanship Scheme, ACUS Umpire/ Scorer courses, other relevant Training courses (Team Manager etc.)

Activity Programmes (Club/School Link Projects) Start up and/or running costs. For example Holiday Coaching courses, Kwik cricket and/or Proficiency award courses, Local festivals/competitions, New Junior and Women's sections/teams.

Small Capital Projects For example wheelchair access, showers or toilets. Other items include Non-Turf Pitches for both practice and Match play (only for ECB approved pitch systems).

Community Capital Projects for grants over £5000.

Priority Areas Initiative (PAI) This fund makes special provision for areas of urban and rural deprivation. For projects that meet the criteria, up to 90% of the cost of new capital facilities can be met by the fund. Potential projects should fit in with the priorities of the ECB, County Cricket Board plans, and local authority plans particularly those likely to cost more than £100,000. Each must support actual participation in sport.

Other fund agencies include: School Community Sport Initiative, Playing Fields and Community Green Space, Community Revenue Projects, School Sport Coordinators, Active Sports, World Class Fund, New Opportunities Fund, The Cricket Foundation, County Cricket Boards – Small Grants (applications to CDO direct). The Foundation for Sport and The Arts, The Lord's Taverners, Institute for Sports Sponsorship – Sportsmatch (*see* chapter on Fundraising), Local Authorities – including County, City, Borough, District and Parish Councils. Rate Reductions and Relief, not a funding but by reducing a club's costs it can be equally as effective in easing a club's financial position. The National Playing Fields Association, Landfill Tax and the Women's Sport Foundation. PLUS The Coalfields Regeneration Trust, The Neighbourhood Renewal Community Chests, Regeneration and Rural Development Agencies, European Social Fund.

Charitable Trusts There are many charitable trusts throughout the country, which have funds to allocate to worthy projects. There are a wide range of organisations from National Organisations from National charities to local trusts each with their own specific criteria and budgets.

Breweries Many breweries are willing to give substantial loans or even grants towards the cost of improving social facilities in clubhouse and community centres. If an existing supplier cannot help, it may well be worth trying rival companies. Start by contacting your local brewery.

Funderfinder This is a small charity that doesn't make grants itself, but provides software that helps groups identify charitable trusts that might give them a grant. This might be available from your local library free or through a local development agency – the software is called 'Apply Yourselves', this can be downloaded from Funderfinder's website:
www.funderfinder.org.uk, from April 2002 they have had another software package called 'Budget Yourselves'.

4 Club Constitution

Policy

When a club is formed, it will set out its constitution – which will include:

¶   The Aims of the Club.

¶   The Club Rules including details of Committees.

¶ The type of Club – Village, League, Friendly, Wandering, Pub, or Town.

¶ Age Groups.

¶ Associations. All clubs should consider being affiliated to their County Association so that they can be part of a parent body that will help with fixtures, leagues, insurance, ground problems etc. It is not a good idea to go it alone.

¶ Who can play – Male and female players are welcome.

Aims

There are a variety of reasons that a club might identify.One could be to enter the club cricket league system and aim to win the top league, alternatively it might wish to be the breeding ground for new talent.

Some examples follow:

THE FORTY CLUB – provides cricket for experienced cricketers over the age of forty years. With the aim of taking cricket to the schools. Endeavouring to encourage schoolboys to play cricket in the spirit of the game, both on and off the pitch. Including turning out properly attired, having a disciplined approach both individually and collectively, properly captained and playing to the highest standard possible. Winning if possible, losing gracefully or if humanly possible making the game a draw, if winning is out of the question. After the match learning to discuss the finer points, so that the utmost enjoyment can be gained from the camaraderie of competition and friendship of opposition, whatever the result.

THE BAT & BALL C.C. – This club has two aims: To keep the famous Inn (The Bat & Ball) closely associated with cricket *in perpetua*. To support Youth cricket in Hampshire.

Most clubs would describe their main aim as to be providing competitive cricket for their members.

Club Rules

The club rules will include:

¶ How the club is set up in terms of club officers: President, Hon. Chairman, Hon. Secretary, Hon. Treasurer, Hon. Fixture Secretary, Hon. Membership Secretary, Chairmen of Sub-committees etc.

¶ When the Club financial year starts and ends and when the AGM will be held annually.

¶ What quorum will be required for meetings.

¶ The formula for creating new members.

¶ How a member can be expelled from membership.

¶ On what grounds an Extra-ordinary Meeting can be called and by whom.

¶ How rules can be changed and by whom.

¶ The level of charge for subscriptions and match fees.

¶ The method of election of club officers and President.

¶ What are the club colours?

¶ Which officers can be signatories for club cheques.

¶ If the Club forecloses, what happens to the proceeds.

The Type of Club?

Whether it is to be representing a town, village or a 'wandering' variety, the latter is a club that plays all their matches on other club pitches. If they own their club and ground, they will need to determine whether they want to play in a league or play declaration cricket.

What Affiliations the Club wishes to have?

Most clubs have an affiliation with the ECB or their County Association, as this will help them to obtain a more economic insurance policy.

5 Membership

Every club depends on good membership for its survival. Initially the club management will devise the method on how members are elected.

It is helpful for the membership secretary to have a formal application, so there is always a record in writing as to when the member was elected.

With the demise of cricket being played in so many schools, it is now very necessary for local clubs to have a junior policy for young members, coinciding with a coaching programme (see 'Clubmark' scheme).

The ECB have a special grant system-providing funds for clubs that have a youth policy. Properly planned this will also generate much needed funds. Moreover, the youth policy will provide future cricketers for the adult teams, without which clubs are unable to survive.

Once this system is set-up, the club should encourage a younger member to sit on the committee, firstly, to ensure the adult members recognise the needs of the younger membership, and secondly, training young members to learn the criteria of how a club is managed.

The committee will set membership subscriptions and they will become due on the same date each year (Their organisation will be under the supervision of the Treasurer),though it is probably better to arrange for the Membership Secretary to be responsible for chasing up bad payers (every club has them). It is a good idea to have a final date for receipt of dues, after which late payers either pay more, or alternatively, they might not be selected. This latter method may deprive the club of players and be detrimental to the quality of team performance, the player leaves and goes to another club.

The manner, in which younger members are handled, is vitally important. Due to their general lack of finance it might be more beneficial to offer them a subsidised, yet bulk figure spanning the five years from 17 years of age up to 22. This keeps them committed to your club, without burdening them and risking their absence due to lack of funds. In special cases their parents might pay on their behalf.

Another method for helping funds and gaining club commitment, is the introduction of 'Life Membership', this can be based on a number of years subscriptions, in most clubs the figure of ten years gains the reward, whilst at the same time giving the club funds a healthy boost. There is always vital committee work for those in the twilight of their careers, so the next stage, in the club terms, is to offer long standing committee members the honour of 'Life Vice-Presidents' or make the 'Life' part only, after five years as a Vice-President. Some clubs use the term 'Vice-President' as a means of inviting local prominent citizens to join the club and pay an annual contribution.

When an individual has given the club special service, the committee might consider honouring the person with a free status. This might be life membership, or a 'Fellow' or another term of their choice. In order to make it exclusivity, it should be stated, in club rules, that there should be only so many at any one time, otherwise it belittles the award.

Match Fees

Every club should recognise the value of members who give their time to represent the club, even though the members gain their own values from the commitment. The match fee has to reflect covering the costs of the game, whilst being not too expensive to deter those members who play regularly. In the future it might be considered, to bring in a sliding scale, to encourage those who play the most.

Cricket Coaches

As Club cricket has taken over the role of the school in the development of young cricketers, every club should endeavour to encourage more senior members to take courses to become cricket coaches. The benefits are considerable and are outlined under another section (Training and Coaching), therefore it is advised that the committee supports the initiative by paying for course enrolment.

Groundsmanship

Not all clubs can afford to pay a groundsman, so that members take on the role. Their training and education can be both encouraged and enhanced through the club becoming a member of the Institute of Groundsmanship.

Through the IOG they can gain valuable experience and information, through their attendance of specific lectures and training courses. They should also try and attend SALTEX, the leading exhibition held at Windsor Racecourse, in September (*see* Note 2, p.138).

We started this chapter by stating that the management should look after its membership. When members stop playing they should not be ignored, for many like to feel they can supply much needed experience and continue to support the club. They can always be used in a variety of ways, such as selling raffle tickets, acting as stewards during important matches, umpiring and scoring, writing the club history, taking photographs, or looking after the bar - all activities that save the club money and help it to run more efficiently.

6 Fund-raising

Every club at some time requires to create new finance. This section provides readers with a wide range of methods. These will range from 'funding' for capital projects, such as building projects, ground equipment – sight screens, artificial pitches, netting systems and scoreboards, to 'funding' for running the club, special events, and even increasing funds for major repairs and maintenance factors.

Before planning how to raise money it is necessary to determine how much is required? If the project can be linked with a specific item, it is much more likely you will gain support for it.

Major Funding for Capital projects

The Committee should decide who is directly responsible to head the team. This person will then need to form a small team to look after the different methods being used to gain the funds.

From the people initially described as officers of the club, the team should include: The Chairman, the Fund-raiser, the Entertainment officer, the Publicity manager and the Press officer.

Methods

1. The section on Grants & Applications for Funding will be the first approach.

2. Most requests for grants will ask 'What money has the club already raised?' This is where the other methods of Fund-raising are required. A lot will depend on the size of the club, the wealth of members and how hard the members and organising team are prepared to work.

For instance, the Club might appeal to members, asking them to make donations. But if the members are mainly made up of young people, this would not work.

One favourite promotion is the 'Sportsmatch' method, A cricket match is arranged and the club gains a sponsor for a specific sum. The Government Body might agree to put an equal amount up as to the amount offered by the sponsor. (*see* Note 3, p.138)

At such an event, one would plan to have celebrities 'giving' their time to support the project and instead of giving them expenses you would need to promise them publicity.

Alongside the event, you might arrange club members to provide a corporate hospitality 'tent', where local companies would be invited to bring their 'Business' guests/clients and you charge them an overall cost per head. This to include – lunch and tea, the enjoyment of watching quality cricket, an opportunity to meet the players, obtain autographs and a programme (brochure) increasing your profit. (*see* Note 4, p.123).

The event programme would include advertisements and might also act as your ticket to the match. (*see* Note 5, p.124)

Dependent on your catchment area, it might be able to gain support from local people 'Buying a Brick'. For this to work you would need to find someone to draw the building planned and number the bricks, put a specific cost per brick and also provide incentives of say, five bricks for the cost of four or ten for the cost of eight etc.etc. Either for individuals or for companies. Then you would need to keep a record, so members and visitors could view the record book in the future.

Alternatively, if it is the wing of the Pavilion you might gain a company to sponsor it in return for being called 'the TimeLife Wing'.

It would be necessary to show the sponsor 's company could use the facilities, invite them to the launch ceremony, ask the company's Managing Director or Chairman to perform the opening, or provide photographs of the launch and have one framed for the company. Gain publicity in the local papers and local radio and television.

Another method is to look for a 'special' angle, then contact a celebrity to act as Patron for the appeal, and write to both individuals and organisations, using the Patron's name to beg for donations. Start a 'Book' and record who has given a donation (*see* Note 6, p.125)

Another method to raise large funds is to create 'Friends of the Club' (*see* Note 7, p.126).

Smaller Fund-raising ideas

¶ Raffles

¶ An Auction

¶ Coffee Mornings

¶ Bring & Buy

¶ Guy Fawkes Bonfire Night (*see* Note 8, p.126)

¶ A picnic in conjunction with an inter-club single wicket competition or six-a-side event. (This is a good opportunity to include young members of the club and their parents)

¶ Barn Dances with a disc jockey.

¶ A Dinner with a speaker/s.

¶ A Ball (*see* Note 9, p.126).

¶ A Race Night (*see* Note 10, p.127)

¶ A sponsored 'Walk' – for walk you can substitute many other factors, the main operation is to include as many of the members and their families as possible, trying to gain sponsorship monies from people outside the club. Make it a day-long event, so those who cannot attend in the morning can participate in the afternoon. Ask the local brewery to give you a barrel of beer, probably arrange it for a day just before the season starts. Involvement is the 'key' to success (*see* Note 11, p.127)

¶ Sales of Prints of your ground (*see* Note 12, p.128)

For all fund raising events, let everybody know for what your club needs to create the funds. Give both members and friends plenty of warning so they, in turn, can plan their participation. Organise each event carefully, have somebody in charge, and ensure each team of people know what its responsibility is throughout the day. It might be necessary to have more than one team of helpers.

If an inter-club event, have responsible people contact members to ensure everybody has received details; the best method is by telephone, gaining as many as possible. Keep a record of those who are going to take part. Try to ensure the President and Committee members are involved. Your event may require money to be spent BEFORE the day or night; thus it is imperative that the organiser keeps in close contact with The Treasurer and keeps a tight control on the expenditure.

It is vital that funds increase; thus it is desirable that publicity should be editorial press releases NOT advertisements, for they cost money.

For Clubs who own their ground:
They may consider it is possible to have hockey played during the winter on the outfield, or youth five-a-side football, thus paying for groundsman's fees during the winter months.

Another method of accruing regular funds is having a Golf section, for many cricketers play golf and they all have friends who play the game.

Four or five 'Golf Days' out of season can raise up to £1000 a year. Many cricketers play golf once they have retired from cricket, in consequence each golf day can bring together current members with those who no longer play cricket and it is an added benefit for the senior members of the club.

During the winter some clubs play table tennis as an alternative sport, helping to keep fit and keeping club members together all-year-round.

7 Relocation of the Cricket Club

Much of the information already supplied on creating a new cricket ground will apply. However, because you are moving your club, it is more likely that your new ground will be larger than the first, and the site has been agreed. The cost of setting up will be to a pre-arranged budget.

Hence it will be vital to include the latest techniques and meet all the requirements of a modern sports club.

PLAN Cricket

Every new, or existing club, has the opportunity to take the advice of a County Pitch Advisor. These are available, through contact with the County Cricket Development Officer. All Pitch Advisors have been trained by the Institute of Groundsmanship

If a youth policy with junior teams is being adopted, then the IOG will probably authorise the installation of an artificial pitch, which might be free.

Naturally the County Planning Officer will be consulted at every stage and when discussing the position and design of the pavilion his advice should be invaluable.

Do not expect any builder to understand the requirements of building your pavilion. At an early stage speak with your insurance advisor and Crime Prevention officer. Consider access for all utilities and services.

The designers of the pavilion should consider position, layout, usage by all the community, including the disabled and both sexes. Design should include thoughts of Building Maintenance, Health and Safety, Security and Storage. Other factors such as fire precautions, or whether a scoreboard is going to be part of the pavilion, are very important if costs are to be kept to a minimum. The design of the scoreboard should be discussed with the manufacturer.

All funding and grant applications are described in Chapter I. During building and ground preparation it is important to have a responsible and well-informed 'clerk of works' to supervise the work being carried out.

Do not try to cut corners; it is likely to turn out far more expensive.

Although not mandatory, check with the Survey department future plans for the area – any new roads, building of estates – grants for infrastructure, houses that might be built adjacent to the ground. Find out about drainage of the area, underground springs, and factors concerning any floodwater in the area.

8 The Value of a Website

a. What can a website do for your Club?

¶ It is a tool to help run your Club more efficiently, economically, and quickly.

¶ It saves time, hassle and effort.

¶ It will help spread the administrative burden across various members of the Club.

¶ It will allow instant access to all details and achievements of the Club, and individual players.

¶ It will create an online almanac for your Club including as much historical data as is required.

¶ It can also help generate extra revenue and additional sponsorship.

b What sorts of sections might you consider in a website?

Home Page

¶ A good site becomes an expression of a Club and its member's achievements and aspirations.

¶ The Club title, colours, crests and photographs.

¶ The Club venue.

¶ The History of the Club.

¶ The Club Officers and Committee.

Fixtures

¶ It will manage all the Club's fixtures in a single application, displaying all the season's games according to team, date, type of fixture or result.

¶ It will provide a team selection process, selecting and notifying the players, and publishing the team on a noticeboard.

¶ It will provide fixture venue details, with addresses, maps, and directions.

PLAN Cricket

¶   Via various website links, it will provide weather forecast. It will provide a scoresheet – either with bare details, or as a classic full scoresheet.

Statistics

¶   It will automatically track all players' records allowing for a full scrutiny of performances to date.

¶   It will enable comparisons across teams' performance, comparisons across seasons and group analysis.

Members

¶   It will store membership files online, including members' contact and playing details, their biographies and their playing record.

Club Administration

¶   It will store details of Club affiliate members, umpires, scorers, and caterers.

¶   It can not only record Committee Minutes, but may provide alarms so that deadlines need not be missed.

¶   It will provide Member Notice-boards, to allow Club information to travel faster than before. Banter Boards, allowing members to chat and exchange information, are also possible.

¶   The website can be designed to recognise certain categories of user and site areas, enabling the Club to determine who has access to what using a basic security matrix. In this way, and using set default security levels across the site, the Club can establish how much information is available to the general public and how much is restricted to Club members or committee members.

c   Where do I get one from?

At the time of writing there are some bespoke cricket club website designers in the market place. Their templated websites will provide all of the above – allowing the Club customer to customise the site to suit his own needs and requirements. Examples of such companies are:

www.play-cricket.com
www.hitscricket.com (*see* Note 13, p.128)

From a website designer, who would design a site specifically to meet the Club's stated requirements. This approach is likely to be more expensive initially than the bespoke approach. Both approaches will levy annual maintenance charges.

d   Do I need one?
¶   More and more people nowadays have access to the Internet, and use it.

¶   Using Internet and email will undoubtedly speed up the process of Club administration, and it will save costs – especially for instance in postal charges.

¶   A website does enable international public worldwide access to your Club's existence aspirations and achievements.

¶   It is still very necessary to educate Club members to access and read the website information and to answer emails. Humans are fallible – if they won't answer letters, they probably will not answer emails.

¶   A website will not run the Club for you, but it will make the running of the Club easier and it should enable/facilitate better communications between administrators and organisers.

¶   It will save administrative time, But will still require administrative effort to maintain the contents of the website absolutely up-to-date. This is normally a daily task – for out of date information on a website is just as bad, poorly accepted and gives a bad impression to the reader as does out of date information on the Club noticeboard.

PLAN Cricket

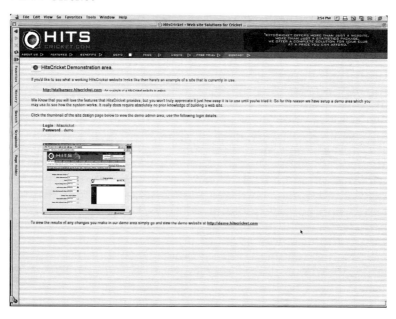

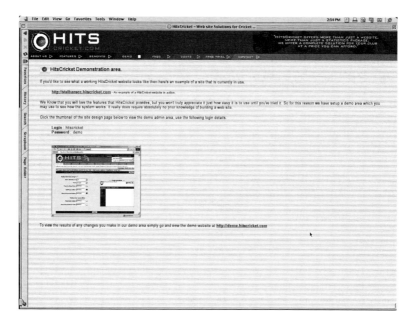

e   Is there anything I can do now?

¶   Yes – get onto the web and have a look at any number of other Clubs' websites, either those on the specialist systems detailed above, or those with their own website. Read and scour them carefully for hints, good design, utility and ideas. Opposite are two windows from the 'hitscricket' site showing its demonstration area and the site of St Albans CC which it hosts. Below can be seen the 'play-cricket' home page of the ECB.

The website designer is always likely to tell you that you need one, because he stands to gain from the deal. Only you can decide if your Club really needs a website.

3 Cricket

Club Image: *Clothing and Leisurewear, Badge, Colours, Club Products and Memorabilia* · Cricket Equipment: *For the club and individual* · Tours & Touring *in the United Kingdom, Europe and Long Haul Destinations; how to organise your own tour or who can organise it for you* · Training & Coaching: *How to meet the Clubmark standard; Course on learning the art of Grounds manship and becoming a cricket coach.*

1 The Club Image

This section introduces the reader to the many varied types of playing and leisure wear now on the market in the form of ties, caps and sweaters all bearing a Club logo and Club colours. There is also a selection of track suits, rainwear and hosiery as well as T-shirts and fleeces.

The Chairman and his new committee will be engaged for hours trying to select the best club crest and colours. Usually they will relate to the local area, either geographically or historically. But they must also do some research to be sure that they do not copy other clubs in the district. The final decision should be simple but effective aiming to keep the end cost within reason and, of course, make repeat orders more likely. The more goods that the club sells to its members the bigger the turnover and the better the profit.

It is worth considering having a player's tie and a member's tie (sometimes known as the city tie). As the Club matures and undertakes tours a further touring tie can be produced but its design should, if possible, always follow the theme of the originally selected club colours.

PLAN Cricket

Beware of acquiring too many different products in stock, ordered too quickly, slowly create your stock, researching first to find out if the item will sell with your members. Bulk orders are cheaper. Some manufacturers might be prepared to accept a large order negotiated at a keener price, but only make and supply the club, as they are needed(*see* Note 14, p.128).

All items created will be another factor in raising club funds, though when reselling to members, remember that overheads need to be added, e.g. cost of administration, cost of despatch, promotion costs and a reasonable profit. Material is another important factor, this will be determined by the overall cost, some clubs decide on either rayon or silk or both – consult both members and your tie manufacturer.

If you have junior members it might be worth considering a junior set of products. It is important they feel part of the club, without having to find too much of an outlay, this will depend on both their age and whether parents will be paying for the items. Also junior clothing has no VAT, thus a reduction in cost!

For cricket caps, there are now many variations – The cap design should include the club crest and involve the club colours. Caps can be in quarters or roundels, or in one colour. The material of the peak should be decided, whether woollen or of the new cheaper style that fits all. Care should be taken that the cap does not shrink, can be cleaned and we advise you talk with the manufacturers regarding the problem of sweat. Before finalising your order, talk to the members and work out the sizes.

Cricket sweaters do not, in the main, carry the 'club' crest, but rely on the colours. For long sleeve sweaters, the colours will be on each wrist and in the 'V' neck and on the sleeveless just on the 'V' neck. There are two other factors to consider, whether the sweaters are in pure wool material, or acrylic yarn or a mixture of them both. Pure wool are the most expensive and warmer, however the 'weight' of the material is important, as a heavy acrylic can offer recipients a happy compromise.

Cricket shirts can either have a placket or button right down the front. There are also three styles of sleeves, long with button or elastic cuff, three quarter length and short sleeves.

It is normal to have the club crest over the left breast, if you have a sponsor their name/ logo goes on the right breast and/or on the collar.

Sponsors in Test Cricket carry their sponsor on the leading arm, but this has not reached amateur cricket yet. Clubs might decide to celebrate a special occasion, anniversary, or reaching a final of a competition by designing a new shirt for the event. As so many clubs either forget to order or do not plan till the very last moment, endeavour to book your order in the autumn or even early winter.

The means of creating club identity through cricket clothing is to have the garments printed, embroidered, stamped, pre-woven or heat-sealed. The length of the run (number of garments required) usually determines the process used.

Leisurewear often chosen include T-shirts, sweatshirts and just recently the fleece has taken over as pride of place. This has become a favourite because of fashion, warmth and use in other sport scenes.

With younger aged groups, the bulk purchase of training wear is another form of product used to create club identity – the garments used to be tracksuits, these changed to shell suits and now various tops and trousers follow the same theme, though rainwear variations have become the norm.

Other club memorabilia may include bow ties, braces, waistcoats, cuff links for men and 'squares', scarves or pins or club favours for ladies. Another item is club umbrellas.

When the club tours they will create clothing that identifies each member of the tour as part of the club. Club plaques are an economic method of providing a present for opposition clubs.

Note: When contacting companies marked in the Reference Section, please ask for the particular products for which your club might require, it will be impossible to mark all products made by each company).

Having your own club clothing enhances club identity and pride in membership. Eventually you will find that, particularly when touring, that your ties and shirts will be in demand from oppositions and one can use them as presentation gifts.

2 Cricket Equipment

Every cricket club that has senior and junior teams must purchase Club equipment and Personal Equipment. Most cricket manufacturers supply these products and we suggest clubs ask them for their catalogues and price lists, before purchase. All the main companies are listed (see Note 15, p.130).

The Club equipment refers to:

Cricket Equipment for Club use

¶ Stumps and bails and heavy bails

¶ A batting-cone for putting rubber handles onto the batting handle.

¶ A wooden mallet for knocking-in bats.

¶ A stump gauge for positioning the stumps on grass pitches.

¶ Umpires' coats.

¶ Bat care products: sandpaper, bat oil and batting tape.

¶ Scorebooks or loose leaf sheets.

¶ Bowlers markers

¶ Umpires counters.

Personal Equipment for Members:

¶ Long and short handle bats and junior size bats for both right and left handed batsmen.

¶ Left and right handed batting gloves

¶ Left and Right handed batting pads.

¶ Adult and junior helmets in adjustable sizes, enough to cover all teams, and for every junior team at least three helmets.

¶ Wicket-keeping pads and gloves for both adults and juniors.

¶ Cricket balls for match play, practice, and coaching.

¶ Cricket Luggage – Team cricket bags for all teams in the club.

¶ Body protection and supports for both senior and junior teams.

3 Tours and Touring

There is no greater camaraderie than that gained from going on a well-organised cricket tour. The formula for success is fairly simple, but it is vital that everyone knows the total plan from the outset. The organiser and his team of helpers must make sure each member receives an equal share of the tour as a whole.

Firstly, this chapter will explain the method of how to organise your tour, as well as offering alternative activities that will enhance the enjoyment of those that will not be playing cricket, or playing in a specific match. One of the most important factors is to arrange fixtures with teams of a similar standard.

Secondly, it is necessary to ascertain the standard of accommodation that the members of the tour require.

Thirdly, the method of travelling to your headquarters and what means of travel will be adopted once you have arrived at your main destination.

Finally, our chapter will discuss the alternative values of various travel and tour organisers who can arrange your tour professionally. This will include what the company will expect from your club and what guarantees you require to make sure they are doing a proper job, and knowing what the company will expect your club to provide.

Tours arranged for the following locations:

¶ To various parts of the United Kingdom

PLAN Cricket

¶   To different Countries throughout Europe and the Mediterranean.

¶   Long haul flights to the main cricketing Countries throughout the World.

How to organise your own tour in the United Kingdom:

Decide whether you wish to travel to a different part of your own country or to travel overseas. Find out how many people would be interested in going on tour, experience usually reveals that an initial excursion will feature sunshine in a holiday environment for a period of one or two weeks. If those who have indicated they would like to tour have chosen more than one tour location, the tour organiser can plan itineraries for each location and cost them separately. Usually once this has been done, there will be a majority decision as to which tour will be chosen.

If you have enough people seriously wishing to tour, then choose a responsible manager, it will be helpful if the person in question has had experience in touring, and he in turn, should choose a sub-committee of helpers. Write out a list of all those who say they would like to tour. It is now necessary to plan when you intend to travel and how many matches will need to be arranged to meet the demands of those making up the tour. As everybody pays the same amount it is important they all play the same number of matches.

Start planning as early as possible. If it is your club's first tour, then you should start organising the tour at least eighteen months prior to when you depart, it is advisable to always have as long as possible in the planning stage, as every piece of research is invaluable.

The tour leader, or one of the sub-committee, should if feasible, make a visit to the area concerned and meet secretaries of potential opponents, hoteliers or view alternative accommodation. Other factors to consider are supporting areas of interest, such as shopping centres, nightlife for the younger element, golf courses, breweries and general entertainment.

Many tours take place without the area being reconnoitred. If the area is not known, close liaison must be made with someone that does know or who lives there.

When costing the tour, include:

¶ Collective travel to the destination (unless tourists travel in their own cars).

¶ The accommodation plus breakfast.

¶ The cost of travel to and from matches for the team.

¶ Match fees including meals taken with the opposition.

¶ The cost of cricket balls.

¶ The cost of the umpire/scorer and their match fees (unless players stand-in).

¶ If you are creating tour clothing, you will need to consider what items will be most popular. Maybe a monogrammed sweater, shirt or 'Tour tie' etc. Once your tour committee has decided, all tour members must purchase the item/s.

¶ The cost of a club plaque or club tie given to the opposition in memory of your visit. If these items are too expensive, an alternative could be a photograph of your touring party pictured in front of your own pavilion.

¶ It is a good idea to have a miscellaneous fund to cover administration – unless the Treasurer agrees that being a 'Club' event this cost is taken from 'general' funds. It would be useful to include the Treasurer in your sub-committee, even though he might not actually be on the tour.

All other extras are the personal responsibility of the individual.

The tour organiser should have access to a computer and email, as this will save both time and expense and ease the communication requirements. Many cricket clubs now have a website so this can help in your research. Contact the local Tourist bureau for more information. Contact the County Cricket Development Officer, who in turn, will supply League and club secretaries. County and League handbooks are another source of information. Past copies of the September issues of The Cricketer magazine will provide lists of accommodation, including addresses and telephone numbers.

Confirm in writing all your fixtures, your accommodation and travel arrangements.

Ensure you know whom you should contact at each club on your touring list and check before leaving that the club is expecting you. Ask them to send their fixture card to you and send them your fixture card. This gives you all their club officials and extra points of contact in an emergency.

At this point, you should have confirmed with all the tour party that they are committed to tour. They should have paid a deposit – say, a quarter of the cost. This will be only returned if a serious emergency occurs. It is advisable that regular payments are made so that everybody is fully paid up well before you embark on the tour, for the tour organiser will have had to pay deposits on your accommodation well in advance of the tour.

Some general points:

¶ Impress on your tour members that they are ambassadors for your club. Any unruly behaviour will mean an immediate expulsion from the tour and a report to the club general committee. Theft or damage to the hotel or place where you are staying will be the responsibility of the perpetrator. Hotels usually report such matters to the police.

¶ All Tourists should have their own insurance – for travel and illness/injury and their luggage.

¶ Similarly, if you are staying at a hotel, you should have some consideration for the enjoyment of other hotel guests.

¶ Remember that your opposition, when playing on weekdays, will probably have taken a day off from work to play against you. It is not only important to play the match in a sporting manner but after the game to stay at the club and spend money at their bar before returning to your hotel. If you are going to be very late, let the hotel know. This is very important if you are expecting them to provide late meals. Use your hotel bar as well.

¶ The best guide as to behaviour is to think how your club would like others to behave with your club, if they were visiting you.

¶ Finally, in case of emergency, find out which hospitals have an accident and emergency department, before you start your tour. Take a medical kit with you for minor emergencies. Find out if anyone on the tour has any medical training.

¶ Provide everyone with an information pack. This should contain the name and address of the hotel /accommodation where you are staying (including telephone numbers), plus the tour fixtures and their locations, with contact names and telephone numbers – in case of bad weather and, Inform them of any planned club event during the tour that they are expected to attend; Finally the tour leader's mobile telephone number.

Most hostelries accommodating sporting groups have an alternative schedule for rest days and rain-affected days.

It is advisable to ask before you finally confirm your booking. These may include clay pigeon shoots, visits to bat making companies, as well as arranging golf, swimming both indoors and outdoors. They will advise on activities for the not-so-energetic tour supporters, including shopping centres, saunas and local craft centres.

Organising your Tour Overseas

When touring overseas other factors are required. All members of the tour party must have a passport, ideally valid for over six months after your tour has finished. Depending on the Country being visited, everybody might require a visa. It is a good idea for wives/girlfriends to be part of the tour, treating it as the family's holiday. Group rates save on the overall cost. Days off are far more enjoyable and everybody learns the fun places to visit. Contact the leading tour operator for the Country, obtain a costing on the duration of the tour and learn all you can from him. You will probably find that the holiday would be better if you book with the tour operator than doing it yourself, this applies particularly to the Caribbean.

Arrangements have to include the mode of travel when you arrive in the country of your choice. It is advisable to have several alternative sets of wheels. Depending on the size of the party you might wish to have a minibus and the use of hire cars which may allow those not playing in a match to choose where to spend their spare time. Usually they will want to arrive at the match for the evening after-match socialising.

It will be necessary to arrange net practice facilities and find out in advance those who might wish to play golf or other forms of entertainment. Usually your hosts will be keen to advise and help you make such arrangements.

If your tour is during the winter months you will need to practise prior to departure and several indoor net sessions should be organised, which are always useful in building-up team unity. It is usual that single males share two to a room and so vital that pairs are compatible.

Before departure on your tour it is wise just to make contact with the teams you expect to play. It is a very great disappointment if you expect to play and for some reason the match is cancelled.

Contact the European Cricket Council website for European clubs addresses.

Every cricket tour should consider having a Tour Brochure. What to include in the brochure:

¶ The front cover will state where your club is going on tour. It should include the club logo and possibly the club colours, the guide is to keep this simple and impressive.

¶ Inside, it is a good idea is to have a forward from the Club President.

¶ There should be a small photo of each tourist and a 'pen-portrait' of each person including nicknames.

¶ The itinerary of the tour can also be featured.

¶ Most important it should carry advertisements from local supporters, from the Club bank, from the company from whom you hire your coach/minibus, and from those companies that supply the club with any product. As an incentive to tourists to help them to sell advertisements, it is suggested that if they sell more than one page they can gain a reduction on the cost of their own payment. All monies going into the 'Team Pool'.

¶ If flying overseas the Airline will usually take the back page. A short club history might also be included. Distribute the brochure to members of your opposition.

¶ Depending on the Country to which you tour, it is worth talking with them prior to embarking. To find out if they would like you to bring cricket equipment with you for them to purchase, you must try and buy it at trade price and sell it on at a profit.

Touring in the United Kingdom

Tours in the UK can be more flexible than those arranged further afield, simply tourists can join the party for either specific matches or stay for just part of the tour. This is an organiser's nightmare and can lead to a lack of harmony. However, it sometimes might be a necessity if you are to have a full side for all your fixtures.

Every tour should have two or three people who make up the

selection committee, one of whom is the Captain. Teams should be picked the night before the game and include a twelfth man, plus umpire and scorer.

The notice board displaying the arrangements should be advised to everybody and then there can be no confusion. Details as to when to assemble are also vitally important. To arrive late at a fixture is very bad manners and unforgivable.

Every tour should have a 'fines' committee, extracting amounts from individuals for semi-humorous reasons, the results being that most people pay a similar amount. The proceeds go to a special last evening' Dinner. After every match the 'fine' manager of the day will discuss with his committee who is to be fined. This may include the opposition and will surely involve those not playing cricket.

Overseas tours

Extra advice to make the tour more enjoyable:

¶ Delegate responsibility to senior personnel – Have a 'Tour Treasurer', a 'Baggage Manager', a 'Vehicle Manager' and a person who can look after any legal disputes.

¶ Arrange for some members to keep tour diaries and to write reports of the matches played for the club history.

¶ So luggage can be easily identified, have coloured tapes attached to each item of tourist luggage.

¶ Arrange for a Tourist party photograph to be taken.

¶ If you intend staying a few days at different locations within the overseas country, playing against several teams at each centre, consider holding a small cocktail party on the first night of arrival, inviting one or two dignitaries from each club you are playing. This will be much appreciated by your hosts. If this exercise is decided upon, it must be costed and included in the tour budget.

Most Countries have tough regulations concerning 'Drinking and Driving', so it is vital that you always work out a list of drivers who in turn abstain from drinking, so everybody can return to your hotel after a match safely.

The Tour Organiser, or his deputy, should always write to the opposition after every game, or directly after he has returned home to thank the opposition for the match and the hospitality received.

Finally, arrange for a get-together approximately one month after the tour so everybody can compare his or her notes and photographs.

Additional factors for overseas tours:

¶ Most international airports have departure taxes. These must be ascertained and added to the individual tour cost.

¶ Matches played in some European countries are played on hired grounds, the hire cost will be shared between both sides, in some cases the ground has a reservation cost or deposit, organisers should check before confirming the fixture.

¶ In Europe some clubs/ grounds do not have pavilions in which to change, this needs to be checked.

¶ Another factor in Europe is that most clubs play on matting pitches, so alternative footwear without studs is required, make sure all players have the correct footwear.

¶ English cricket balls may wear out more quickly in overseas conditions. It is advisable to purchase Kookaburra cricket balls, which are the most used throughout the world, outside the United Kingdom.

¶ When playing in very hot countries, players are advised to take salt tablets at breakfast before playing. 'Twelfth' men should carry salt tablets, a towel, and high-energy drinks with them for the drink intervals. If your team is batting, then each batsman might require a change of batting gloves.

When choosing tour operators it is essential that they are suitably bonded, ideally with ABTA, ATOL and IATA. This ensures that your money is safe.

Professional Tour Organisers

United Kingdom

If you prefer to have your tour organised in the United Kingdom there are two types of company who will prepare your tour for your club.

The first will make all the arrangements and add on an administrative cost.

However there is one company – Shire Sports – that will not charge your club anything for arranging the tour, moreover they will obtain a greater discount on hotel charges than you could obtain. They make their profit by receiving an even better rate from the hotels.

If you engage a professional organisation to arrange your tour, they will need to know your standard of cricket, the type of accommodation you require, for how long you require to be on tour, how many matches you wish to play and what other activities you require to be included? They will need to know the size of your party and how many are married?

Whichever organisation you engage each will require a non-returnable deposit per tourist.

The most important factor is to book your tour early, particularly if you intend touring to a popular tourist area; opponents can only take so many days off to play visiting teams. Keep regular checks on the fixtures arranged and confirm independently with your opponents that the date stated is correct for them.

All fixtures should be confirmed prior to Christmas, the year before the tour takes place.

Overseas

Cricket is extremely lucky to have some excellent Sports Travel companies who provide overseas tours to almost every cricketing destination. Most of them are very experienced and have arranged so many tours to each destination that your club will be delighted with the results. Most clubs taking long haul tours will travel through a professional tour operator. They will obtain group travel rates, which will be linked with the accommodation charges. The rates will be much cheaper than if you were travelling individually. If required they will arrange internal flights; and in some cases have local travel managers on site to ensure the tour is successful. If the tour is travelling to a regular cricket tour destination, their experience will be invaluable. However your tour organiser will need to liaise carefully to ensure that the opposition is of a comparable standard. This is not easy.

The leading companies are Gullivers Sports Travel, Sport Abroad, The Sporting Traveller, The Cricket Tour Company, Sun Living, Paragon Sports Management, Living with the Lions, Rumsey Travel, and Titan Tours (*see* Note 16, p.131).

Always try and do some research of your own, for instance through contacting the International Cricket Council Tel: No. 020 7266 1818

You will be able to find out the address of each Country's Board of Control, from whom you can ascertain the main clubs in the area you wish to visit.

Valuable information on the country being visited can be gained from the internet. Everything known in advance is valuable, even finding out details about the general behaviour. A visit to the Country's embassy is an advantage. Finally warn everyone to be careful in packing their own luggage and never take a parcel for someone else.

The major Sports Travel companies will have specialist trained personnel for specific venues, e.g. Norman Davies is Gullivers Sports Travel manager for West Indies and he has made countless tours and led thousands of happy tours to the West Indies. Another similarly experienced is Richard Webster of Sun Living. For the best tours choose the professionals, it will mean you guarantee that your tour will be successful.

4 Training & Coaching

How to meet the Clubmark standard

Considering this subject, we felt that the subject matter would simply cover the training of groundpersons and cricket coaches. However, our research into club development uncovered -

'The Sport England Clubmark scheme' set up by the England & Wales Cricket Board (ECB) in conjunction with Sport England (Sport England is the brand name of the English Sports Council which is a distributor of Lottery funds to sport in England). This we feel is of such importance that the scheme process should be described at the beginning of this section.

The National Strategy for Cricket, published in 2001, set out seven independent steps that are critical to the development of the game from the playground to the Test arena. Cricket clubs play a crucial role in this – particularly in the role of nurturing young players.

The Clubmark scheme is therefore seen as an important initiative designed to ensure clubs receive the support they need to develop their junior sections.

How your club benefits from Clubmark accreditation

Clubmark will benefit your club by:

¶ Promoting your club
¶ Giving support from sports professionals
¶ Increasing membership
¶ Developing your coaches
¶ Developing your volunteers.

Clubmark will be used to set the standards for a network of cricket clubs providing a safe, effective, child-friendly programme for their juniors.

Clubmark forms the foundation of the club accreditation scheme, providing the core standards that all clubs will be supported to achieve. In addition, it is anticipated clubs will be further recognised where they demonstrate one or more of the following:

¶ A programme with schools and other community groups
¶ A coaching and competition programme
¶ A player development programme for talented players.

Promotion and Support

Through the network of County Boards, Cricket Development Officers (CDOs) and Sports Partnerships, support and advice will be available to clubs involved in the scheme.

Benefits are available to help develop, promote and sustain a vibrant club development programme. CDOs will advise clubs if they are in a position to progress to one of the three ECB Development Club categories.

*(For further information clubs should contact your CDO, details from either www.ecb.uk or by telephoning ECB on 020 7432 1200. Plus special thanks to Ed Leverton – Club Development Manager for ECB)

The Accreditation Criteria

'The Duty of Care and Child Protection'

The Club must work towards full implementation of the ECB child protection guidelines and two members, one of whom must be a coach, have undertaken recognised child protection training.

It has adopted codes of conduct for all coaches, officials and volunteers working with children and young people.

There is access to first aid at all coaching, games and match sessions and there are emergency procedures for dealing with serious injuries or accidents. The senior club official has a telephone access at all times whilst the children are at play or training.

The Club has the contact details for all its children and young people and they have gained knowledge of all their relevant medical conditions and advised their coaches on a need-to-know basis.

Coaching and Competition

The Club provides a structured and regular coaching programme as well as using ECB resources to enhance training and the evaluation of programmes. All playing members are offered match play opportunities. They have at least one active Level One coach and the ratio of coaches to players is not greater than 1: 16. * All coaches should hold professional indemnity and/or professional liability insurance.

All coaching, competition and games need to take place with safe equipment and in a safe environment.

Sports Equity and Ethics

The Club will require an open, ECB approved, constitution and adopted the ECB sports equity policy and/or its own policy. One member must have attended a Running Sport A Club for All workshop and a coach has attended a **sports coach UK** Equity in your coaching workshop.

The club has codes of conduct for parents/carers and spectators, as well as the code of conduct/set of rules for children and young people.

Club Management

The Club must be affiliated to the ECB and carry a Public Liability insurance. It will require a specific membership category and pricing policy for children and young people. Other requirements include:

A system communicating Club Officers with both members and supporters.

There is a nominated junior development co-ordinator, heading a recruitment strategy not only for children and young people, but also for parents and carers. *It is vitally important for the Club to have a 12-month action/development plan in place, which is reviewed by the Management Committee on an annual basis.*

Elvaston Cricket Club is one of the first clubs to have received accreditation. They kindly have allowed us to describe how they gained their achievement. It is reproduced here for guidance of clubs considering this development. (The authors are indebted to Dave Bull, manager of their juniors at Elvaston Cricket Club).

Elvaston Cricket Club have been running a junior section on and off for around 30 years. This has only been possible because members have been willing to put themselves out by running junior practice and matches. There has been little structure to what was done and little support from the governing bodies of the sport.

Over these 30 years we have witnessed considerable changes within society. Clubs today need to be given support to provide opportunities for young people. Cricket is not a sport blessed with large amounts of sponsorship money. This means that it has to spend its money wisely and target it where it will provide the greatest benefit. Dave Bull writes 'I believe that the ECB Clubmark is one way of prioritising funding that directly contributes to the development of cricket at grass roots level. The clubs that are suitable for Clubmark are the ones that are already developing cricket in this manner. Clubmark should be an aspiration for all clubs who are committed to junior development'.

Whilst Elvaston have been developing grass roots cricket for some time, difficulty has been experienced maintaining continuity. One year we would have 40 children, the next we would have only 10. One year we would have 10 helpers the next year only three. If we were to survive as a club and to grow we needed to develop a strategy that created the opportunity and the infrastructure within the club for the continued and sustained development of our junior section.

In order for this to be achieved we have had to convince the club and its members that an investment in the junior section would be

PLAN Cricket

worthwhile. The starting point of this process was to put in place a junior development plan that gave the club clear aims and objectives. In our case the aim was:

'Provide the opportunity for any junior to play cricket irrespective of ability, race, sex, or disability. To develop junior cricket within the club to enable between 3 and 6 juniors each year, on a rolling programme, to have the ability to play in the adult teams, thus generating a lifelong interest in the sport'.

To support this aim we defined our objectives as follows:

1. Improve safety
2. Encourage individual development
3. Increase enjoyment
4. Provide the opportunity to play competitively.
5. Provide an infrastructure that support the introduction of juniors in cricket.

To implement our objectives we put in place the following strategy:

1	**Improve Safety**
1.1	Coaching to be delivered by trained and qualified people
1.2	Provide suitable equipment
1.3	Provide adequate supervision
2	**Encourage Individual Development**
2.1	Provide a structured and consistent award scheme
2.2	Set individual targets
3	**Increase Enjoyment**
3.1	Provide structured coaching in the disciplines required
3.2	Setting individual and group challenges
3.3	Develop team spirit by introducing fun activities
3.4	Maintain a warm and friendly and welcoming environment
4	**Create the opportunity to play Competitively**
4.1	Organise teams for matches at u-11, u-13, u-15.
4.2	Organise tournaments or participate in other club tournaments

4.3   Give every junior the opportunity to play competitively.

5   **Create an infrastructure that supports the Introduction of Children to Cricket**
5.1   Maintain links with local schools
5.2   Maintain junior sub committee
5.3   Maintain a process to continually support the coaching requirements.

These key issues were put in place five years ago and remain as valid today as they were when we first started. Each year we review our plans, prioritise and reissue. We do not worry about not achieving our plans because we are dependent upon many different inputs. The important thing is to be thinking about what the club wants and planning to achieve it.

Each club needs to make up their own mind about how they want to develop. Elvaston's plans have proved to be a major success. Five years ago we had 20 juniors and were declining, with our better players leaving to join other clubs. Now we have 86, with around 20 juniors or former juniors playing regularly in our adult teams. We even had two juniors playing at Lord's in the National Village final last year.

We have also received an 'Awards for All' grant to support our work delivering cricket in schools, improving cricket skills and introducing a partially sighted cricket club.

The club and membership are now committed to junior development. This has driven the whole club forward and given us a different perspective on how a club can be run for the long term. Our priorities and structure are driven by investment in the future. It is these characteristics that are developed by the ECB Clubmark process. True it may mean clubs that have ECB Clubmark status stand a better chance of grants than those who do not; but the real benefit of Clubmark is the change in culture within the club that results in a vision for the future. Long may Clubmark prosper and best wishes to those clubs that genuinely gain from the process.

* * *

The rest of this chapter concerns the responsibilities of Club Officers for overseeing the Training & Coaching of various members of the club who have a duty to meet some specific standard, whilst carrying out work for the club. Even though they are probably of an amateur status, and act as volunteers, they should try and meet certain standards to carry out their work satisfactorily.

No quality cricketer will join a club without a reasonable playing surface on which to bat. In order that every ground reaches an acceptable standard, The England & Wales Cricket Board in association with The Institute of Groundsmanship has a structured short course to develop the skills and expertise of **Cricket Groundsmen**. The scheme consists of three levels of progressive training offered in four courses.

The initial stages are the Spring and Autumn Practical courses, Level 1 parts 'A' and 'B', followed by Level 2, 'Understanding the science' and culminating in the Level 3 course, 'The Management Practices'(*see* Note 18, p.139).

The outline programme for each course is:

Spring preparation   Level 1, Part A

Early Spring Maintenance; Preparation of the Square; Machinery; Mowing; Rolling; Watering; Scarifying and Brushing; Fertiliser Application; Preparation of the Match Pitch; After-match Pitch Repairs and Renovation; Maintenance of Non-Turf Pitches.

Autumn Renovation   Level 1, Part B

Sequence of Operations; End of Season Repairs and Renovation; Scarification, Aeration; Overseeding; Top Dressing; Fertiliser Application; Care of the Outfield; Maintenance of Non-Turf Pitches; Winter Work. *Both these one-day courses are held at various sites around the counties.*

Understanding the Science   Level 2

Pitch Specification; Soils, Top Dressings, Motty Testing; Grasses; Fertilisers used in Turfculture; Pests, Diseases and Weeds of Turf;

Synthetic Pitches; Machinery and Equipment.

Management Practices   Level 3

Performance Quality Standards (PQS); Pitch Construction; Preparing the Ideal Pitch; Pitch Allocation – The Outfield; Net and Practice Areas; Budgeting – Resources; Health & Safety Management. ECB Club Management and Regulations.

Both of these are two-day courses at specific sites in the British Isles.

COURSE COSTS

(costs include all refreshments, lunch and tuition)

Level 1	£50.00
Level 2 (Course only)	£145.00
Level 3 (Course only)	£145.00

For further information and application forms you should contact one of the following: Your County Cricket Development Officer at the County Cricket Board, or Christopher Costello at the Institute of Groundsmanship. Applications should be sent to arrive no later than fourteen days prior to the commencement of the course. No refund can be made after acceptance on a course.

In order that cricket clubs can progress to a higher standard, they should motivate their members to train to become cricket coaches. Their incentive is the development of youth cricketers who will progress to play for the club when they become adults.

The ECB has set up a new National Coaching Scheme. This sets out a complete programme to which a cricketer can build to become an international standard coach. For the purpose of this book, however, we are only including Levels 1 and 2.

Level 1

This is the highest 'entry level' course in the National Coaching scheme. Its aims are to equip beginner coaches with skills and knowledge required, and to introduce and develop cricket amongst young people in an environment of safety and enjoyment.

Those candidates gaining Level 1 status will be able effectively to introduce and develop cricket skills to young people using group coaching. They will demonstrate a clear understanding of both the principles and content of the ECB Coaches Code of Conduct. Other attainments will include providing effective technical models of key cricket skills; understand the principles of child protection; working with children and NET Management. They will be able to access and deliver a range of skill development drills; arrange and small-sided games, and umpire a small side version of the game.

Level 2

The Level 2 course builds on the skills and knowledge gained from level 1 and delivers further competency in technical modelling and demonstrations, effective communication, sport psychology, biomechanics and physiology.

In teaching the plan and method required for a net session know how to evaluate it, be clear in using video to analyse performance and know emergency first aid. This course will create a coach who can provide effective technical models for all the main cricketing disciplines for batting, bowling, fielding and wicketkeeping. He will either coach, on a one-to-one basis or in the team environment.

Both courses have a duration of 18 hours and will benefit the club as well as the individuals participating. The cost to enrol on Level 1 is approximately £85 and this increases to about £100 for Level 2. This differs slightly depending on the County to which you apply, but it will be in the region of these figures.

Clubs or individuals wishing to enrol should contact their

County Cricket Development Officer.

Anybody coaching in the club environment is strongly advised to make sure they know the principles and content of the ECB's Coaches Code of Conduct.

All ECB Coaches are further advised they should enrol as members of the Association of Cricket Coaches and protect themselves with the Association's insurance policy.

4 External Facilities

Planning a Cricket Ground and Square · Groundsmanship · Ground
Equipment and Machinery · Artificial Pitches

1 Planning a Cricket Ground and Square

The Founder of a new club must first establish what category
will the club fit. Is it to have its own ground or can it lease a
ground? Or, will it be a wandering club playing all their matches
on the opposition's ground.

Most of this book is about the club that has its own base. The
Founder needs to research from where the playing members will be
found, what is the catchment area, the proximity of other clubs
and their strengths and whether the new team will be joining the
league system. This early research will be of great value when ap-
pealing for finance, whether it is club fundraising or attempts at
gaining financial grants.

(Most of the statements in this section will be relevant to the
development of a club, even if it has been in existence for many
years. Every club should have a good look at itself in the current
situation. For in recent years the game and its organisation have
been turned upside down. Every club has to meet new demands of
playing standards and facilities).

If the club is starting with just a playing area, the following factors apply:

¶ The position of the square must be established, with the angle of each pitch in relation to how the drainage falls.

¶ The second consideration is the angle of the sun as it 'goes
down' in the evening; so that if possible it is not shining into the
eyes of either batsman. (Clubs can gain advice from their Cricket

Development Officer, who in turn, will put them in contact with their Pitch Adviser and the Institute of Groundsmanship)

¶   Once the position of the square has been defined, the next step is to establish if the boundaries are of sufficient length for the standard of cricket envisaged. The optimum length should be in the region of 75 yards. One needs to attempt to create an oval effect.

¶   As with the second point above the positioning of the pavilion – from where club officials and the teams will be watching the game is important. If possible spectators in the pavilion should not to have their enjoyment marred by having to look directly into the sun.

Positioning will be largely determined by access to water and electricity (and possibly telephone lines), and the nearest points of these to the property.

Every extra yard the club requires to obtain access to these services is unnecessary cost. Particularly important is main drainage and natural drainage, although obvious, it is sometimes overlooked that water runs better downhill. When establishing a new ground it is easier to lay an under ground pipe to the square during construction than doing it later. This eases the groundsperson's problems for when repairing and creating pitches during the season.

The stopcock should be located off the square, below the ground surface. Remember to insulate the piping so it does not freeze during the winter and break under the ground.

Another factor to be considered at construction stage is the installation of an artificial pitch. (*see* Note 18, p.139). This can be very helpful (if placed on the side of the square – on the dry side), as it is very useful for young cricketers to learn by playing on a true surface with consistent bounce. Moreover, they will not wear out the important strips being used for the senior team matches.

Never try using club members to install an artificial pitch, bring in the experts; if it is wrong you have someone to blame and you can make them get it right. In many cases the Institute of Groundsmanship will supply a pitch free.

The quality of your cricket pitch is probably the most important single factor throughout the cricket club's history. For capable cricketers will not play on bad pitches. Gaining good facilities (even though the cost might be high) is the best investment any club undertakes. The capabilities of the Ground's Director and groundsperson are vital for the success of the club. It is advisable to include ongoing training as an expenditure item for the groundsperson.

2 Groundsmanship

Although we have talked about the ground in general, this section deals with the more vital requirements of pitches and outfield and their maintenance. The Laws of cricket dictate specifically the actual measurements for adults and junior cricket (Law 8). For this book we describe the requirements for adult cricket only – further information can be obtained from the Institute of Groundsmanship (*see* Note 17, p.133).

Other requirements from the Laws:

The pitch should be 22 yards long and 10 feet wide. The Laws state area of the pitch (Law 7.1) the width of the stumps how they must be pitched (Law 8.1), and the stumps sizes/bails (Law 8.2).

Most amateur cricket clubs have to rely on volunteers to prepare and maintain their pitches and outfield. This work is probably the most important activity, for everybody's enjoyment will depend on the quality of the surface they prepare. Initially, the County Pitch Adviser should be approached through the County Development Officer. He will provide invaluable information as to the steps to be taken to determine how the square should be laid out.

PLAN Cricket

For an existing square it is always advisable to have an interim assessment from the professional. In most cases this will be free, and this can be ascertained before making the appointment.

Cricket squares should be 'laid down' with a life expectancy of twenty five years, and the size of the square will be determined first, by the size of the ground, and secondly by the number of matches that need to be played upon it in any one season. As a benchmark any one pitch can have up to five matches played upon it. A north/ south layout is preferable but an East /West variation of 55 degrees from the north point is acceptable.

The indigenous soil must be identified for its texture before any construction is started. It is normal for soil samples be taken from six different points before soil analysis is taken. Both topsoil and subsoil should be analysed.

Care must be undertaken when establishing a new ground not to allow heavy laden construction vehicles to access the pitch; they may do untold harm to the outfield, especially when damp or soft. Also beware of using cheap ground materials, for they will cause future problems and in the long term cost far more than the initial savings.

Suitability of the topsoil will be determined by its clay content, probably between 25-30%. Grasses and seed mixtures will be determined by the balance between the ideal type of grass and the maintenance that will be carried out. Every year the Sports & Turf Research Institute (see Note 17, p.139) publishes a list of 'Turfgrass Seed' showing the various types of cultivars of the different species available.

Consolidation of the square is the most important factor. Professional advice should be taken as to how this is carried out, and regards levelling and seeding. Similarly professional advice should be taken in determining how the after care is maintained. This also applies when recreating a new pitch within an operational 'square'.

3 Groundsman's Equipment

The equipment below lists the minimum recommended items required to maintain a cricket pitch in a safe and consistent condition. Some of the items, if not owned by the club, can be borrowed or hired when particularly needed.

1. Mowers

¶ Pitch Mower – This should be cylinder mower (with no less than eight blades, capable of 130 cuts per metre and no wider than 600mm, variable speed and collection box) suitable for pitch/square preparation, with adjustment tools.

¶ Outfield Mower – They include trailed or mounted gangs, width 1.8 – 2.1m or, ride-on, width 1.2 –1.8m.

2. Rollers

¶ Hand Roller – This is the light roller with a eight ratio of 75 – 250kg with a width of 0.6 – 1.0m

¶ The Heavy Roller, ideally will be self propelled, but there are various makes that can be used using a tractor or car for propulsion. The medium roller should be up to 500kg or heavy roller up to 1,016kg – width 1.2m

3. Scarifiers

¶ Hand – width 68cm.

¶ Self Propelled – will have an operating width of 35 – 50cm, a 5hp engine and tines: thatch control/ thatch prevention/brush.

4. Aerators

¶ Sorrel Roller – with a width of 900mm –1.2m with solid tines 37-50mm, set spirally along the drum.

¶ Pedestrian/self propelled – Hydraulic ram – With a width of 1.0 –1.2m and a tine depth of 75 – 100mm and tine spacing of 50 –100mm and 75 to 100 holes per square metre.

5. Fertiliser Distributors

¶ Belt – 61 – 92cm

¶ Cyclone/disc – 1.2 –2.4 distribution pattern.

6. Pesticide Applicator

Knapsack/ walk-over sprayer (groundsman must be qualified).

7. Setting Out Equipment

¶ Tape Measures – 2 x 30m, 1 x 50m, 1 x 100m.

¶ Lines – 2 x 50m.

¶ Pegs – 12 x 150mm (minimum)

8. Marking Out Equipment

¶ Straight Edge – 1 x 3.6m

¶ Marking Frame/ template

¶ Paint Brushes/ line marking material

¶ Boundary marking equipment/ material.

9. Irrigation Equipment

A system to get water to the square in sufficient quantities.

10. Hand Tools

¶ Springbok rake

¶ Wheel barrow

¶ Switch/whale bone brush

¶ True lute

¶ Drag mat/drag brush

¶ Besom broom/ stiff brush

¶ Stump hole marker

¶ Hammer

¶ Wooden mallet

¶ Setting bar

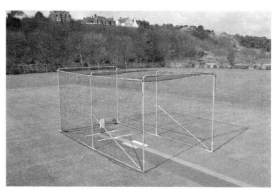

¶ Shovel

¶ Fork

¶ Tool kit

¶ Bucket

¶ Thumper/ heavy spanner

¶ Several germination sheets.

(Source: TS4 – *Recommended Guidelines for the Preparation and Maintenance of Cricket Pitches and Outfields at all levels of The Game*. ECB in association with the Institute of Groundsmanship).

4 Ground Equipment

This section considers Artificial pitches, Boundary markers, Boundary netting, ground protection netting, Pitch covers, Scoring Systems - Scoreboards/ Fascias/ Boxes, Sight screens and water removal machines. Practice net systems.

Germination sheets and maintenance of all equipment.

Ground equipment for many clubs used to be considered as a luxury, but with the introduction of the many grants available it has become the necessity if clubs are to be accepted into the higher leagues. Without the satisfactory ground products promotion is declined.

The ECB initiatives for providing clubs with youth sections to qualify for new funds through the Clubmark challenge will soon go further, the more the clubs are prepared to improve their facilities the more they are likely to receive support.

Club Groundsmen and Ground Managers should always talk with the manufacturers of the various products they require as every pitch/ground has a different need. Currently it is often factors apart from cricket alone that may decide why one product will fit the requirement more effectively than another. The main difference will be the standard of cricket played, the size of the club and the purchasing power in finance terms.

Therefore each product will be described, but there might be smaller or larger models available.

Boundaries

Boundaries used to be marked by white plastic flags, which tend to break. Blocks of wood with a large nail knocked through it do equally as well (these should be painted white). Many clubs have followed their County counterparts by obtaining a long rope, as it saves a lot of time for the groundsman and is far more effective in the long term. If flags or their alternatives are used, then a white line has to be added; if moved this can cause confusion and does not look professional. Where grounds have fields surrounding them, the edge of the ground will either be a fence or hedge, in which case the club should either purchase chicken wire netting or buy ground netting (*see* Note 19 p. 139).

Clubs surrounded by houses and gardens need to consider the purchase of high protective netting (*see* Note 19, p.139). However this is a costly exercise. The dangers mainly depend on how close private property is to the playing area. If there is a problem, try and deal with it before going to court; friendly neighbours and courteous behaviour are far less expensive.

Pitch Covers

These may simply be flat plastic sheets with eyelets along their edges for pegging down – many companies can supply this type (*see* Note 19 p.139). The next step is to have the same product attached to a roller, with wheels (*see* Note 19, p.139) at either end - enabling the people to quickly put on the covers and remove them. The speed in putting them on is probably the most important factor, especially while a match is in progress.

Roll-on covers are made by most of the ground equipment companies (*see* Note 19, p.139). They are available in a variety of styles, most are with pitched roofing in the middle or a slope from one specific edge. Nearly all have a galvanised steel base, which will not rust. The covering material may be plastic sheets, but some have a treated waterproof canvas. One design is of glass fibre construction that is virtually vandal proof. Every design includes attached hoses, running water away from the covered pitch. Wheels are a vital factor, as unless they are made of rubber, they are likely to damage the square when it is soft or wet. These can easily puncture, so ask about this before signing the contract, and find out the remedy if they do puncture. There is one design that has the opposite style, that of a concave shape, with the water draining to the end of the cover, down the middle, which dispels the need for guttering (see Note 19, p.139). Some models have a domed shape.

In order to cover the pitch and bowlers' run-ups companies supply either three or four covers, depending on their measurements. When clubs order covers, all these aspects should be checked and they should insist the covers are assembled – (from an insurance viewpoint it is a good idea to have them chained together when the ground is not occupied). Similarly, if a tow-bar is connected the groundsman can attach them to a tractor and wheel them in to place easily. The wind factor needs thought, not only from being blown away or the covers being lifted, but also whether rain will blow under the covers, (again talk with the manufacturers). Many covers can have hooks attached to the sides and extra sheets attached. Your covers are not only as protection against rain. When the weather is particularly cold you can use them for frost protection; and in very hot summers they may prevent the pitch from becoming too dry.

Two companies supply covers that will cover either the whole square or the whole ground or part (Note 20, p.142). Such a system is unlikely to be used by a club, unless it is a professional ground.

Scoring Systems

The range of scoring systems is enormous, with many different varieties.

PLAN Cricket

They start from the portable that is like a large suitcase. When opened it acts as a temporary board, useful when playing on council sports grounds (Note 21, p.139). Next is the free-standing blackboard style on which numbers hang on hooks. This has been improved upon with the use of levers on the side of the product and clearly shows the scores (Note 21, p.139). Instead of a scoreboard attached to the pavilion, many clubs have a separate scorebox, in which the scorers can sit away from distractions, but more importantly sheltered from inclement weather (Note 21, p.139). Most boxes have numbers attached to strings that flip over when pulled. The scoring system that is becoming more and more popular is the electronic scoring system. This enables the scorer to sit almost anywhere on the ground, with the keyboard and at the push of a button show the spectators the scores on the scoreboard. This method has the added advantage that the scores can easily be printed off and records of averages, analysis and information supplied instantly. Clubs with this facility can also promote advertisers' messages and gain valuable revenue throughout the match (Note 21, p.139).

Sight Screens

The basic design is white canvas stretched between two poles and pegged down in one place. These are immovable during the game but will be put in the pavilion and stored between matches. For many years most screens were made of solid wood painted white or duck egg blue and mounted on wheels, but required several men to push them into place. These have the disadvantage of being blown over in a strong wind, tend to rot as they are out in all weathers throughout the year and are a natural target for vandals. Other designs have been developed, including sight screens that can be either folded or dropped down to half the size when not in use. Also certain companies decided that by using specially treated wood they could guarantee far longer life to the wood variety. Further development changed the wood for plastic and instead of being a solid screen they would alternate white plastic slats, thus allowing for a percentage of the wind to pass through the screen, the full screen being mounted on wheels.

Some other styles are now available, one company designed a screen that had a galvanised base with steel wheels (stationed outside the boundary so will not damage the ground). Upon this they had a galvanised rectangle of tubular steel with a white canvas sheet lashed to it.

Although this could be removed between matches, on most occasions it was left out throughout the summer. It was more likely to blow over, but was easily pushed by one man. Based on the galvanised surround and base they then introduced a roller at the top of the screen, onto which is wound a white nylon net with a close mesh. This can be unwound before the match and locked in position. Thus allowing 30% of the wind to permeate through the screen, this reduces the risk of it being blown over. Also by retracting the net back onto the roller at the end of the match, it becomes virtually vandal proof and windproof and is easy to move by one man. Out of season the roller with net can be removed and stored away. There is nothing to rot or rust (Tildenet Retrax). Wooden screens are still the least expensive. They have the versatility of being made to much larger sizes than the new models.

Water Removal Machines

If pitch covers are of the lay-flat variety, there is a problem of how to remove the cover without spilling water onto the pitch you have covered.

The sure method is to take the water off first. Several motorised and pedestrian models are capable of carrying out this task. Each machine has a roller in the front covered by a sponge-like material that soaks-up the water and deposits it through a squeegee into tanks placed behind the roller. When the tanks are full the machine is taken to the boundary for emptying.

PLAN Cricket

Netting Systems

The simplest method is still to have one or two nets supported by poles and pegged down by guy ropes and pegs. On the other hand if many wish to practice at the same time you require a more sophisticated system. This has to be flexible as every few days the net sides must be taken-up for the Groundsman to mow all the pitches. Some have poles that fall into sockets; in others the netting hangs from wires. Some companies have designed and produced a mobile net that runs on wheels and can be moved to different parts of the ground. This is particularly useful if one wishes to practise on the square or on an artificial pitch. Most of all it has the value of practising without playing on the same area time after time and so removing all the grass.

Germination sheets

After every cricket match has been played on a pitch the bowlers' footholds need repairing. The procedure used to be sweeping away all debris, watering and sprinkling grass seed and fertiliser and hoping. Now by using germination sheets of closely meshed netting, the process is speeded-up considerably. Repairs or creating new grass quickly is much easily achieved, saving the groundsman heartache.(Available only from Tildenet Ltd.)

If your club requires details for any of the products we suggest you ask for several quotes.

Maintenance

Before all your ground equipment is dismantled ready for storing it should be thoroughly checked, moving parts cleaned and greased, ropes examined for fraying, strings and scoreboard items looked over, hose pipes coiled and stored. This is good practice and will ensure everything is in good order for the new season. Any item showing deterioration can be repaired and put in order. With some pitch covers the manufacturers will carry out the cleaning on your behalf.

5 Artificial Pitch Purchase and Installation

Every club that either leases or owns its cricket ground will consider the values of purchasing a non-turf (artificial) pitch . This chapter also applies to many schools who will be in the same position. Artificial pitches are used for both practice areas and match pitches.

Practice

The preparation of practice net areas is both costly and time consuming.

For most clubs such areas are small in space and in a corner of the ground, just outside the boundary. It does not take long before all the grass is worn away and it only takes a shower of rain and the ground becomes unplayable. Therefore net practice areas benefit enormously by the installation of an artificial pitch. This is effective unless the ground is underwater and requires little or no maintenance from the overworked groundsman. Moreover, the same pitch can be played upon day in day out without the facility ever changing. It is an even greater bonus for younger players who need the ball to have consistent bounce so they are able to 'form' their strokes without the fear of unexpected 'rising' balls.

Instead of a full pitch being purchased, the usual arrangement is for a separate batting end and a bowling end to be installed, if more than that, then multi bays are supplied. With some companies they will supply the full complex. There are several styles – these are usually only required by sporting complexes rather than an individual club. If required ask the manufacturers.

PLAN Cricket

Match Pitches and Material laid for Practice Areas

In this section we describe the various forms of artificial pitch, the values will be respective for both match pitches and the practice ones.

We asked the five leading companies to describe their products which appear in alphabetical order – for addresses and contact details (*see* Chapter 6, Note 18, p.139).

Installing an Artificial Pitch
by Keith McGuinness, Club Surfaces Ltd

Pre-1976 'non-turf' probably meant a slab of concrete and coconut matting. Unreal and, worse, potentially dangerous. The quiet revolution – the simple but brilliant concept of 'natural' non-turf pitches – was, however, gaining momentum at this time.

The concept was to construct a pitch base that would replicate the changeable playing characteristics, dependent on moisture content and compaction, of a natural pitch. Surfaced with a high quality woven artificial grass, the pitch would sustain constant use with a very low maintenance requirement.

The now famous Club Turf Pitch was convincing early visionaries such as Tom Cartwright, then Manager and Coach at Glamorgan, of its potential contribution to the game when he broke new ground at Sophia Gardens with the first such dynamic-based practice pitches installed at a county ground.

The rest, as they say, is history with Club Turf Pitches now installed at Lord's and other famous test arenas around the world and, probably of more importance, some 5,500 pitches installed at less illustrious clubs and schools.

Development and sophistication are now such that a temporary Club Turf Pitch can be installed at the Millennium Stadium for international day/night matches and earn plaudits such as 'a great all-round cricket pitch' from Wasim Akram.

At the conclusion of his wonderful career Derek Underwood chose to put his experience and reputation into non-turf pitches and joined the Club Turf team in 1988. Derek is adamant that this is a specialist field. 'You cannot', he says 'take chances with cricket pitches and put them in the hands of sub-contractors. Whether Bombay or Birmingham, Club Turf Pitches are installed by our own permanent staff'.

Sound advice from the expert – and the non-turf scene can be a minefield. Whether a single batting end, multiples of practice pitches or a match pitch on the edge of the square, the advice has to be to call in the experts who 'invented' the concept back in 1976.

A Club Turf match pitch will probably cost, net of VAT, between about £5200 and £6200 depending on type and size, the standard lengths being 27.0m and 30.0m. Installation, utilising specialist plant, is normally completed in one day, and work goes on year-round – the Lord's pitches, for example, were installed during December.

A normal practice pitch configuration is 11.0m batting ends and 8.0m bowling ends, although full-length 27.0m or 30.0m pitches are very much on the increase.

Another feature that is gathering momentum with practice set-ups is synthetic carpet infills surrounding the pitches within the netcage area in order to eliminate awkward grass-cutting maintenance.

A budget price example for two batting/bowling ends practice pitches, netcage and synthetic infills would be about £12500.00 - £13000.00 plus VAT

Derek Underwood will visit your club to advise on siting, ground levels and conditions, prices and all-aspect of non-turf pitches.

Installing an Artificial Pitch
by M.H.Percy, Exclusive Leisure Ltd

Exclusive Leisure have two ECB approved systems, one has a hard porous base and the other a tarmacadam base, this is known as the 'T' Base system.

Both systems are covered with the Tom Graveney Cricketweave surface, this carpet is of woven Wilton construction.

The specification for the Tom Graveney Cricketweave Match pitch is as follows: The quotation is based on the assumption that the installation is carried out on flat and level ground and does not include for any remedial work or 'marrying in' to the surrounding ground. The artificial pitch will be installed to correspond as near as possible to the existing levels of the surrounding ground.

The installation would include first the removal of the existing turf and top soil to a depth of 115mm (this would be left on site for further use/disposal). Then a pressure treated timber edging would be fixed around the perimeter, upon which graded aggregates would be laid in the base to a depth of 75mm. Next,

Hard porous material would be laid to 40mm, this would then be rolled and consolidated. During this process stump boxes would be put in place and filled with clay/soil. Over the bowler's run-up a 7.5 mm thick shock pad is incorporated. Finally the carpet is fitted to the whole area, stretched and secured by stapling into the timber edging. The final process includes the cricketweweave being stretched and secured by stapling into the wooden surround.

Alternatively, the installation specification of a practice facility using the Tom Graveney Cricketweave with the 'T' Base system would receive the same preparation, based on the same assumptions.

We would remove the topsoil and turf as per the Match pitch and fix the same treated timber surround. Similarly, the graded aggregates would be laid and onto that our 'T' base system would be laid comprising of the special tarmacadam, this is then rolled and consolidated. Over this surface we supply and lay our intermediate pad. Finally, the exclusive Crickeweave artificial grass is fitted over the area of each batting and bowling end, stretched and secured by stapling into the wood surround.

Recent installations include practice facilities at Repton School, Rugby school and Malvern College. Whilst our new Actionpitch cricket surface has been laid onto concrete bases at Millfield School.

Tom Graveney is still actively involved and lends his name to endorsing pitches in support of the England and Wales Cricket Board initiative to provide quality match pitches to clubs and schools. The Cricketweave wilton carpet is available in lengths of 30 metres and widths of either 2.74 metres or 2 metres.

Every pitch is installed by our own experts.

Some of our clients include Durham, Leicestershire and Worcestershire County Clubs and Eton, Cheam, Repton and Rugby schools. Our products carry all the normal guarantees.

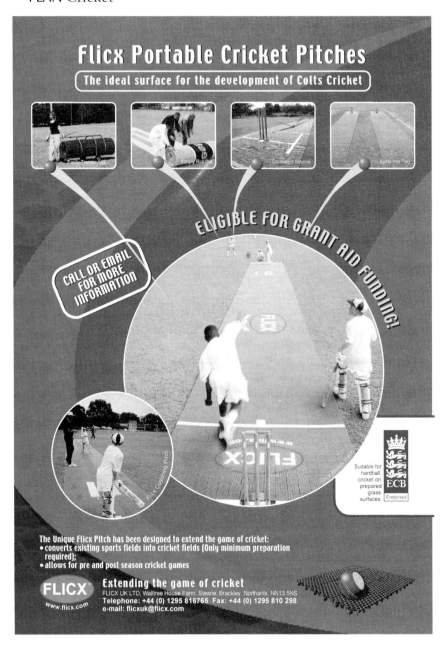

The Installation of an Artificial Pitch
by Gerard Farnham, Flicx (UK)

Flicx Cricket Pitches is an integrated system of synthetic surfaces which offer schools and clubs versatility in whatever training or matchplay environment they have available.

The whole concept of Flicx was to enable those with limited facilities to be able to quickly facilitate football or other sporting field, into a cricket field with a cricket pitch mirroring the true qualities of bounce and dependability. This achieved, Flicx has developed their product to either integrate with the grass growth or provide alternative variations to help the coach 'in the middle' or in the nets during practice. There are three separate styles: All green for Matchplay (Roll up and Roll Down – can also be split to be used in two nets) –

Skills, with positions marked for batsman's feet for specific strokes, and Coaching, specially colour coded to support the coach.

Installation
The Flicx Match pitch may be laid flat on an existing cricket pitch or square, the only preparation required being to mow, scarify and cover with either clay or topsoil and rake flat before rolling out the pitch. Flicx Pitches are supplied in two halves that knit easily together – what is more, when the pitch is left in situ, it allows the grass to grow through it and (as long as the mower is kept flat) it enables the whole surface to be kept mown.

Whenever anyone is handling the mat itself, everybody should wear gloves.

Flicx Pitches measure 25 metres by 2.5 metres wide.

In order that the layer knows where the mat should be split in half, there is a white triangle painted discreetly on the mat. Each mat has two straps, which are laid out on the ground before rolling up takes place, these will be parallel to each other. Roll from crease to centre, keep in place by linking the strap around the coiled mat, and engage the locking buckle and press down. Do not carry the mat, but use the carrying cradle this is placed over the rolled mat and two moulded hooks link into the straps and the cradle can then be easily wheeled to your store room. Now unhitch from the cradle and store with the

101

pitch on its end, this keeps the mat in good condition and takes up very little space. Ensure nobody ever sits on the rolled up pitch. As already explained the mat is in two sections, if required for net practice, each section can be placed separately in each net. When rolled out flat, each end should be secured at each end with 4 or 6 inch nails. The creases are also nailed into position.

If your Flicx Pitch needs its position adjusted DO NOT try and pull it sideways, but roll it up and then move it.

Flicx pitches can also be used on a flat school playground or any flat surface.

Half sections can be purchased separately.

All the range of pitches are competitively priced, there is an excellent video showing the products versatility and various uses, alternatively visit the company's website: www. Flicx.com

Installing an Artificial Pitch

the notts sport® way, by Richard Tigwell, notts sport®

With twenty years experience as one of the leading specialists in the design, advice and supply of artificial surfacing – from cricket to multisports and children's play areas – notts sport® is the real project enabler, working to provide solutions for the local community.

When planning to install new non-turf cricket facilities, take full advantage of the notts sport® tailored pitch design service.

The reason for purchasing a non-turf cricket pitch, for match or practice can be very different from one organisation to the next. A school for instance may be looking to replace poor grass facilities. A club may be looking to accommodate a growing junior section or an increasing number of society games. A small village may be looking to start a new club. Therefore, one needs to ensure that the new pitch will play in a way that is suitable for the age and ability of the players.

There are a wide variety of non-turf pitch systems available today and offering different playing characteristics, life expectancies and maintenance levels. In addition to these factors, the condition of the proposed site evenness, gradient, drainage and consolidation) must be taken into account if a new pitch is to be constructed correctly and play successfully.

A careful choice is needed to make sure that the pitch is right for the players and the proposed site. notts sport® is the pitch specialist offering the right knowledge and experience to your project.

Their service for new build pitches includes:

¶ Comprehensive discussion with end users to help establish the types of playing characteristics required. Is it to be used for juniors, seniors or both: for practice or matches: how often will it be used: do you want a consistent performance or do you want it to mimic a natural turf strip?

¶ Full technical site survey and investigation of proposed site to establish necessary preparation works, taking into account levels, drainage, access to the site and whether spoil needs to be removed or can be deposited on site.

¶ An agreement of the expected life span and performance parameters required, and an agreed maintenance package/schedule to suit the client needs.

This information is then collated to enable notts sport® to draw a detailed constructional specification that will ensure the new facilities are installed correctly and satisfactorily. A competitive tender process can then be arranged on the designs from a number of authorised notts sport® distributors.

All these distributors are independent sports ground contracting companies who undertake to employ suitably experienced staff trained in the installation of notts sport® designed cricket facilities. Only such companies are authorised to offer quotations for notts sport® designs, and they aim to produce work to the highest standards of workmanship quality and expertise.

The national network of authorised distributors can offer the following advantages:

¶ A local service that is fast and efficient.

¶ Best value on a like for like basis. You have the peace of mind that all the quotes will include the same pitch type and quality of materials – the pitch you actually want. Also grant agencies require you to conduct a competitive comparison for your new facility and the most appropriate quote can be included within your grant application.

PLAN Cricket

¶ Excellent after sales service. Many distributors offer a good range of maintenance packages.

¶ References. Each company will be able to provide a referral list of completed notts sport® designed installations upon request.

Following the installation of a non-turf cricket pitch by one of their approved distributors, they will then issue your pitch warranty and maintenance guidelines.

The warranty is valid for a period of five years for new build pitch systems and covers such items as performance, UV degradation and manufacturing faults in the artificial carpet. The distributor will additionally provide a one-year constructional warranty to give you peace of mind that the new facility has been installed correctly and in accordance with the design specification.

Also, after installation, notts sport® will be on hand to discuss any queries you may have. A selection of their designed facilities is subjected to a post installation-testing programme. This involves a number of tests, based on ECB Board recommendations, being carried out free-of-charge and culminating in a written test report being presented for your information.

Installing an Artificial Pitch
by Bob Cooke, Peak Sports

One of the simpler ways, and the Australian way, of installing an artificial pitch is to lay a 12.5m x 1.83m x 80 mille (deep) of concrete or tarmac and simply glue on a Wimbledon Unreal grass pitch (or nail on in the case of tarmac).

The bounce is near perfect, no upkeep necessary. Examples of these pitches can be seen at Winchester College, who have twenty (20) nets and three full length pitches; Radley College, Ipswich School, Manchester Grammar School, Lancaster Royal Grammar School, Merchiston Castle School, Wellington College, Cheltenham College, Finchley CC, Stockport CC, UCS and Warwickshire CCC. A huge percentage of cricket grounds in Australia have purchased them. The pitches offer a good bounce factor providing batsmen with real practice. Installation is fairly simple, we have found that customers return time and again for repeat orders.

Installing an Artificial Pitch
by Peter Dury, Verde Sports

The Verdepitch Rollup/Roll out Cricket Surface

Tried and tested over a number of years Verdepitch is a roll up/roll out cricket surface suitable for use on any level surface both indoors and outdoors. The height of bounce is dependent on the firmness of the structure on which the surface is laid.

Surface – UV stabilised green needle punched polypropylene providing excellent grip and wear characteristics. This also allows the ball to grip and turn giving encouragement to spin bowlers, a feature often absent from indoor surfaces.

Backing – Heavy non-slip polymer backing providing strength and allowing surface to roll out flat time and time again without curling at the edges and corners. Textured finish to backing absorbs energy and reduces pace off both solid and sprung indoor surfaces.

Size – Verdepitch is supplied 2.00m wide in lengths to suit customer's requirements.

Maintenance – Easy to clean the surface will accept a number of marking materials including paint and tape.

Handling – To avoid injury during handling, it is recommended that the surface is rolled in to position and only lifted by sufficient numbers to suit the size of the roll. Alternatively mobile handling units can be supplied that allow the rolls to be lifted and wheeled in and out of storage areas.

Practice Cages

Fixed Frames – High quality heavy-duty frames are supplied. Uprights are fixed into position, set in concrete and the top of the frame is held together with elbows and grub screws. This means that, if desired the whole structure can be dismantled and stored during winter. Each bay frame measures 3.60m x 3.60m and the length's are to customer's requirements. Various qualities of frame can be supplied.

Mobile Frames – A mobile freestanding frame, measuring 7.20 x 3.60 x 2.70m with two wheels at one end is supplied. Additional braces are included to provide additional stability to the frame during movement.

Traditional timber pole and guy rope nets can also be supplied which

PLAN Cricket

can be used for practice on grass or synthetic pitches.

Maintenance of Synthetic (non-turf) Cricket Pitches

Immediately after installation – All synthetic pitches will benefit from regular rolling during the first few months following installation. This will bed the materials onto the base formation and increase compaction in the sub structure.

Rolling should be carried out with a 5-6 cwt roller to avoid creasing the carpet or breaking up the base. During rolling the carpet may raise slightly in front of the roller but will settle back down once rolling is complete. In the event that a slight rise still exists, this will normally be at the end of the carpet. The nails at the edge adjacent to the rise should be lifted and the carpet allowed to settle.

To prolong the life of a woven carpet fill the pile of the carpet, if not carried out during installation, with fine sand or soil in the bowlers delivery area, extending no more than 0.50m in front of the popping crease on match pitches.

Regular Maintenance

Your synthetic turf cricket pitch will benefit from the following minor maintenance procedures:

During the season –

1. Mark out the crease areas with emulsion paint.

2. Rolling can be carried out throughout the season particularly if more bounce or pace is required.

3. Check the stump areas and ensure the soil is moist.

4. Clear any debris off the surface and sweep off any grass clippings.

5. Cut around the perimeter of the pitch with a cylinder mower to keep the perimeter neat and provide a smooth transition from the grass to the synthetic surface.

6. Check the level of particulate fill in the area of woven surfaces and top up if necessary.

7. Check the surface for spike damage and repair with adhesive as necessary.

End of season

1. Clean off the surface by sweeping to remove any residual dirt or remove soil and seed blown onto the surface during post-season

maintenance of the square.

2. Check for any damage to the surface and repair as necessary.

3. Check for depressions in the bowlers' delivery area and where the batsmen stand. In a few instances the pressure exerted by the bowler's front foot and by the batsmen hitting the surface with his bat can cause small depressions in these areas. In such circumstances the surface and underlays should be rolled back to allow the affected areas to be levelled.

Pre-season

1. Occasionally roll the pitch during the spring, increasing the frequency as the season approaches.

2. If necessary weed and moss kill the surface and sweep off any dead material.

3. If the grass has been allowed to grow around the edges, such that the surface has been pushed in to form a bubble, the grass should be trimmed back and cleaned off the surface. The perimeter nails can then be removed to allow the surface to settle flat and then refitted.

5 Internal Facilities

1 Pavilion Design

Every club that owns or leases its ground will need a pavilion. Initially this might be a modest affair, dependent on finance available. There are many grants to which application can be made for support funding. The success in gaining support will be largely dependent on the efforts of Club Management in their own fundraising.

Pavilion requirements include:

¶ Changing facilities for the teams and umpires.

¶ Showers, wash basins and lavatories and somewhere to include the boiler for heating the water.

¶ Provision of catering facilities for cricketers, umpires and scorers.

¶ Possibly a licensed bar. This will require a bar cellar – remember security requirements and save on the insurance costs.

¶ It is vital to recognise the needs of facilities for both sexes and for the disabled – especially wheelchairs. All grant applications will depend on what arrangements have been included for these sections and this single factor will help to increase your award.

¶ It might include the 'scorebox' and/or the scoreboard fascia.

¶ A box room for storage of tables and chairs.

Actual Design

When planning the precise design for the pavilion it is very important that the sub committee includes the club' officers, an architect and a surveyor. Besides the functional aspects, the end result must fit into aesthetic factors of the area.

Its position we have dealt with, but other factors include 'sky-line views', vehicle access, other buildings, elevation, parking facilities and the size of the building. Once the club officers have made their decisions, an architect will need to make drawings. This will be followed by the submission of the plans to the Planning Officer of the County Council, who, in turn will advise the Parish Council. To each the club should make approaches to ascertain the viability of the project.

When creating a new ground it is advisable to consider the likelihood of future buildings, both for the club and its neighbours. For should a sudden surge of new dwellings be planned, then councils and the environment may be delighted you are creating potential leisure activities for the new inhabitants. Even if there is not a plan, the club should point out that it is improving the current leisure facilities; it does not matter if those living close to the ground are not members.

We have shown the need for careful planning and property design. The latter must also include some thought on what materials will be used to construct the building – particularly how they fit in with the surrounding landscape.

Other factors to be considered:
¶ The size of structure.
¶ The neighbour's views
¶ The building design
¶ Cost
¶ Ongoing and long term building maintenance
¶ NEVER have a flat roof

It is vital for those responsible for the pavilion design to remember that the building (in most cases) will not be inhabited for most of the winter, therefore unlike a house, such factors as condensation and lack of heating must be considered at the planning stage. In such circumstances buildings quickly deteriorate. Other factors affecting pavilions are security, and protecting the buildings them-selves – for many such buildings are located in an isolated position and these days can be an open invitation for vandals to damage for the 'fun element' alone. If the pavilion in question is isolated, there is the extra factor of 'Fire Risk' to be considered – this takes us full circle to rethink what materials will be used to build it.

It is not unusual for the pavilion to have a storage area built-on to include groundsman's machinery and materials. Access from the pavilion is sometimes considered, which puts the pavilion in more jeopardy. It is more advisable to not follow that path.

Once the sub committee/Executive Committee have formed their own conclusions, but before actual plans are drawn up, it is advisable to talk with the relative Council planner to gain their opinion. Each step, made in the correct order will ultimately save time and the club's money. The more advanced the long-term planning, the greater will be the savings. Talk to all the relative agencies, not forgetting the local Crime Prevention officer.

2 Security

Most amateur cricket clubs are located in less populated areas and are therefore potential targets for vandalism and burglary. Whilst obviously covered by insurance it is the responsibility of the entire committee to oversee the security of the premises at all times. Should the worst happen and the club has to make a claim to their insurance be sure that they, in turn, will require evidence to prove that the club carried out their security responsibilities ab-solutely.

Groundsmen's equipment – such as mowers, hand rollers and forks, spades and hand tools are the most vulnerable and the easi-est for the thief to sell, so a secure lock-up is vital. For the pavilion itself, including in many cases a bar, all alcohol or money left on the premises is at a high risk and should be discouraged. Hopefully those responsible for design of the building were aware of the security factors. The pavilion has to be very carefully protected.

Methods include bars on windows, video cameras, excellent locks, steel shutters for the bar area.

Locks that have numerical codes are helpful, as their combinations can be released to only responsible officers and saves the risk of keys being lost. Another factor is to deter the would-be thief by limiting access to motor vehicles when the ground is unoccupied. All security matters should be discussed with your local crime prevention officer and your insurance broker. It is more intelligent not to leave money on the premises and limit the amount of alcohol in storage. Arrange for deliveries close to the date of consumption.

Ensure security for pitch covers and sight screens; the former can be chained together; the latter will depend on their design - immobilising wheels is one option. If thieves or vandals are caught ALWAYS prosecute, if only as a deterrent to others.

3 Fire Safety and Electricity

It is amazing how many cricket pavilions are burnt down. Usually it is when the building is unoccupied, so everyone should always take care when locking up,

Ensure combustible material is well away from potential fire risk items. Make sure all windows and doors are shut, switches are turned off and sky-lights are closed.

YOU CANNOT BE TOO CAREFUL

¶ Make sure all users of pavilions know where the Fire Extinguishers are located and how they should be used. They should be checked regularly and the dates should be logged.

¶ The Pavilion Manager should also make an inventory of all items kept in the pavilion, in case of emergency.

¶ Extra care should be taken if a kitchen is part of the building – For the kitchen it is advisable to have a FIRE BLANKET.

Extra information

If you discover a fire, you will need to act calmly and quickly.
If it is a small fire you may be able to put it out:

¶   Before making an attempt to do so **you must raise the alarm.**

¶   Make sure you have a clear escape route.

¶   Do not tackle the fire if there is a danger of being trapped or if you have not been trained.

¶   Leave the area. Close the doors behind you to help stop the fire spreading.

¶   Leave the building.

Fire action and fire safety signs must be clear. The local fire authority will pay a visit to instruct where these should be placed.

Fire Extinguishers

Foam Use for burning liquids, chip pan fires, petrol fires.

Powder Use for burning liquids, electrical fires, pan fires

Water Use on general fires such as burning paper, cloth and wood

Halon Use of electrical fires and burning liquids

Carbon Dioxide Use for burning liquids, electrical fires and pan fires

AFFF Use for general fires, burning liquids and pan fires

Fire Blanket Use on pan fires, when a person's clothes are on fire.

Electricity

There are three main risks with electricity:

¶   Electric shocks – when electricity passes through the body it causes shocks, burns and can kill.

¶   Fires – Approximately 19% of all workplace fires are started by electrical appliances.

¶   Faulty Wiring – Most pavilions that catch fire involve faulty wiring. Regular checks should be made and recorded as to who made the check and the date.

Ways to avoid the above:

¶   Do not overload sockets.

¶   Keep electrical equipment well maintained

¶   Keep cables in good repair

¶   Never touch light switches or appliances with wet hands.

4 Creating a Bar and Catering Facilities

The first step in creating a bar is to telephone a number of suppliers to find out who will provide the best deal. Some might offer finance in designing the bar in return for your stocking their product.

Many suppliers will be happy to give promotional material, which includes glasses, beer mats, bar towels, umbrellas etc. This reduces the amount you have to pay for these items.

Also ensure that the draymen are happy to put the kegs in the cellar (if you have one) and not leave them outside the premises. It is sometimes more economical to purchase all soft drinks, splits etc. from the supplier. This factor needs to be checked, as sometimes it is less expensive to go to the local Cash and Carry.

It is ideal if all bar staff are instructed how to change a barrel, also how to clean the pumps. This is extremely important as many of the 'funny tummy' experiences are due to dirty pumps.

When setting up the bar, make it as 'user friendly' as possible, you should not have to lean across a couple of spirit bottles to reach the pint glasses, for at some time the bottles will be knocked to the ground. Ensure your till is well out of reach of the customers and notes are kept out of sight. You might be sure of your members, but friends and their friends etc. might not be so trustworthy.

Endeavour to find a retired member to set up a rota system of bar stewards, offer them their meals free and you will find you have a profitable bar. Though it is surprising how many players just forget to pay, in error.

Try not to allow the setting up of a 'tab system' or slate. This works well during the opening times, but unfortunately when it comes to tallying up people forget how much they have drunk.

Make regular stock checks, endeavour to fill the shelves after every match and ensure you do not run out of product. Make a reliable person responsible for the bar and supplies.

Remember to ensure the duty bar steward supplies enough 'float' for each match. Team captains should detail players to help wash up and dry glasses.

5 Health & Safety

CRIMINAL LAW is set by Parliament. If a person breaks the law they can be punished. The police have the power to arrest suspected criminals and bring them to court. In the area of occupational health and safety it is HEALTH AND SAFETY EXECUTIVE INSPECTORS, and local authority ENVIRONMENTAL HEALTH OFFICERS who can prosecute clubs and individuals who break health and safety law.

Expect a visit at any time – you cannot refuse admission.

The following are some guidelines to follow to ensure a good working relationship with the Environmental Health Officers. If they see you are trying to follow the correct guidelines, they are very helpful.

You must remember that it is always your Responsibility – if you are the main person, not the person who brought the food, or those who dispensed it. Or even the person preparing it – it is the operator of the kitchen or bar, who 'carries the can'.

The essentials of food hygeine
¶   The Food Handler should keep clean and wear clean clothes
¶   Always wash hands thoroughly: before handling food, after using the toilet, handling raw foods or waste, before starting work, after every break and after blowing their nose.
¶   Before starting to prepare food, The responsible person must be told about any skin, nose, throat, stomach or bowel trouble or infected wound. Anybody failing to do so is breaking the law.
¶   Ensure cuts and sores are covered with a waterproof, high visibility dressing.
¶   Avoid unnecessary handling of food.
¶   Do not smoke, eat or drink in a food room and never cough or sneeze over food.
¶   Do not prepare food too far in advance of service.
¶   Keep the preparation of raw and cooked food strictly separate.
¶   Clean as you go. Keep all equipment and surfaces clean.
¶   When re-heating food, ensure it gets piping hot.

Adequate provision must be made for the removal and storage of food waste and other refuse. Refuse stores must be designed and managed in such a way as to enable them to be kept clean. Protect against access by pests. Make sure they can't contaminate food, drinking water, equipment or premises.

Competent Persons
Certain health and safety legislation requires the appointment of a competent person. For instance to comply with the Management of Health and Safety at Work Regulations, employers must

appoint competent people to assist with health and safety measures.

The Management of Health and Safety requires every employer to carry out risk assessment. Risk assessment will give a clear picture of how an accident might happen, how likely it is to happen, and how serious it could be.

To do this, employers must: identify workplace hazards, identify who is at risk, evaluate the risk, eliminate or reduce the risk by deciding on control measures.

All accidents must be recorded; and as the serving of food or drink is involved, any disease must be reported to the enforcement authorities. Useful addresses are given in Note 22, p.144.

6 Reference Sections

Note 1
Cricket Development Officers for First Class Cricket and Minor Counties

If the C.D.O. has changed please contact the England & Wales Cricket Board, Telephone 020 7432 1200, who will advise who the new CDO is and where to contact him.

A First Class Cricket

Derbyshire Colin Davies (Secretary)
Derbyshire Cricket Board, County Cricket Ground, Nottingham Road, Derby DE21 6DA. Tel: 01332 388130   Fax: 01332 388133

Durham Nick Brown (Cricket Development Officer)
Durham Cricket Board, County Ground, Riverside, Chester-le-Street, Co. Durham DH3 3QR. Tel: 0191 387 1717 x 2822   Fax: 0191 387 1616

Essex Mike Boyers (Cricket Development Manager)
Essex Cricket Board, County Cricket Ground, New Writtle Street, Chelmsford, Essex CM2 0PG. Tel: 01245 254025

Gloucestershire Mike Bailey (Cricket Development Officer)
Gloucestershire Cricket Board, c/o Dowty Sports & Social Society Ltd., Arle Court, Hatherley Lane, Cheltenham,
Gloucestershire GL51 0TP. Tel: 01242 571213   Fax: 01242 522410

Hampshire Neil Rider (Cricket Development Manager)
Hampshire Cricket Board, The Development Office, The Hampshire Rose Bowl, Botley Road, West End, Southampton, Hampshire SO30 3XH.   Tel: 023 8046 5816 Fax: 023 8047 5618

Kent Jamie Clifford (Director of Cricket Development)
Kent Cricket Board, St Lawrence Ground, Canterbury, Kent CT1 3NZ.   Tel: 01227 456886 x 214   Fax: 01227 473608

Lancashire c/o Andrew Hayhurst (Secretary)
Lancashire Cricket Board, County Cricket Ground, Old Trafford, Manchester M16 0PX. Tel: 0161 282 4127   Fax: 0161 282 4151

Leicestershire Ann Woods (Cricket Development & Promotion Officer)
Leicestershire & Rutland Cricket Board, County Ground, Grace Road, Leicester LE2 8AD. Tel & Fax: 0116 244 2198

Middlesex David Holland (Administration & Development Secretary)
Middlesex Cricket Board, Lord's Cricket Ground, London NW8 8QN. Tel: 020 7266 1650 Fax: 020 7289 5831

PLAN Cricket

Northamptonshire Ian Lucas (Cricket Development Manager)
Northamptonshire Cricket Board, County Cricket Ground,
Wantage Road, Northampton NN1 4TJ Tel: 01604 514456 Fax: 01604 514488

Nottinghamshire David Tighe (Cricket Development Manager)
Nottinghamshire Cricket Board, Trent Bridge, Nottingham NG2 6AG.
Tel: 0115 982 3008 Fax: 0115 981 0304

Somerset Andrew Moulding (Cricket Development Officer)
Somerset Cricket Board, The County Ground, Taunton, Somerset TA1 1JT.
Tel: 01823 352266 Fax: 01823 332395

Surrey c/o Karen Meaney (Secretary)
Surrey Cricket Board, The Oval, Kennington, London SE11 5SS
Tel: 020 7820 5734 Fax: 020 7735 7769

Sussex Steve Peyman (Development Manager)
Sussex Cricket Board, County Ground, Eaton Road, Hove,
East Sussex BN3 3AN. Tel: 01273 827104 Fax: 01273 771549

Wales Mark Frost (Director of Cricket)
Cricket Board of Wales, Sophia Gardens, Cardiff CF11 9XR
Tel: 029 2041 9336 Fax: 029 2040 9390

Warwickshire Richard Cox (Director of Cricket, Recreational)
Warwickshire Cricket Board, County Ground, Edgbaston, Birmingham B5 7QU.
Tel: 0121 446 3615 Fax: 0121 440 8297

Worcestershire Stuart Lampitt (Cricket Development Officer)
Worcestershire Cricket Board, County Ground, New Road,
Worcester WR2 4QQ. Tel: 01905 749447 Fax: 01905 429147

Yorkshire Andrew Watson (Cricket Development Officer, South Yorks)
Yorkshire Cricket Board, 8 Swinston Hill Road, Dinnington, Sheffield, South Yorkshire S25 2SA. Tel & Fax: 01909 565029

B   Minor Counties

Bedfordshire David Mercer
73-75 Harpur Street, Bedford, Bedfordshire MK40 2SR.
Tel: 01234 261391 Fax: 01234 327588

Berkshire Steven Ayres
Berkshire Sports Partnership, 2-4 Darwin Close, Reading,
Berkshire RG2 0TB. Tel: 0118 939 9006 x 6 Fax: 0118 939 9028

Buckinghamshire Stephen Goldthorpe
Bucks Indoor Tennis Centre, Holmers Lane, High Wycombe,
Buckinghamshire HP12 4QA. Tel: 01494 536111 Fax: 01494 536109

Cambridgeshire Russell Doel
c/o Automatic Devices Limited, Langford Arch, London Road, Pampisford, Cam-

bridge, Cambridgeshire CB2 4EE. Tel & Fax: 01223 832244

Cheshire Richard Newton / Peter Hancock
1 Moss Farm Cottages, Moss Farm Recreation Centre, Moss Lane, Winnington, Northwich, Cheshire CW8 4BG. Tel: 01606 871200   Fax: 01606 76800

Cornwall Tim Marrion
Unit 6, Threemilestone Industrial Estate, Truro, Cornwall TR4 9LD.
Tel: 01872 324387   Fax: 01872 324334

Cumbria Bob Simpson
Unit 22, Summerlands Trading Estate, Endmoor, Kendal
Cumbria LA8 0ED.   Tel & Fax: 015395 60066

Devon Stuart Priscott
East Devon District Council, Knowle, Sidmouth, Devon EX10 8HL.
Tel: 01395 517470   Fax: 01395 517507

Dorset Keith Brewer
The Dorset Cricket Centre, Hurn, Christchurch, Dorset BH23 6DY.
Tel & Fax: 01202 470852

Guernsey Mike Kinder
'The Wickets', Sohier Road, Vale, Guernsey, Channel Islands GY3 5PX.
Tel & Fax: 01481 249420

Herefordshire Chris Dirkin
Herefordshire Council, Culture and Education for Life, Grange House, PO Box 44, Leominster, Herefordshire HR6 8ZD   Tel: 01432 260152   Fax: 01568 611046

Hertfordshire
Leisure & Recreation Department, Welwyn/Hatfield District Council, Campus West, The Campus, Welwyn Garden City, Hertfordshire AL8 6BX.
Tel: 01707 357195   Fax: 01707 357185

Huntingdonshire Paul Taylor
Bridge House, 23 Bridge Street, St. Ives, Cambridgeshire PE27 5EH.
Tel & Fax: 01480 461005

Isle of Wight David Killpack
31 Quay Street, Newport, Isle of Wight PO30 5BA.   Tel & Fax: 01983 825462

Jersey Chris Minty
Fort Regent Leisure Centre, St. Helier, Jersey, Channel Islands JE2 4UX.
Tel: 01534 500159   Fax: 01534 500127

Lincolnshire Mark Fell
27 The Forum (1st Floor), North Hykeham, Lincoln, Lincolnshire LN6 8HW. Tel: 01522 688008 (Main Office) 01522 688093 (Direct Line)   Fax: 01522 688073

Norfolk Godfrey Batley
Unit 2, Loddon Business Centre, 2b High Street, Loddon, Norwich, Norfolk NR14 6AB.   Tel & Fax: 01508 522915

PLAN Cricket

Northumberland Ian Wardle
Northumberland Cricket Board, c/o Newcastle Football Development Centre, Gibside Gardens, Benwell, Newcastle upon Tyne NE15 7PP.
Tel: 0191 274 1528   Fax: 0870 132 6333

Oxfordshire Rupert Evans
Oxford City Council, Bury Knowle House, North Place, Headington, Oxford, Oxfordshire OX3 9HY. Tel & Fax: 01865 741393

Shropshire Cookie Patel
Telford and Wrekin Council, Education and Culture, PO Box 211, Civic Offices, Telford, Shropshire TF3 4LA Tel: 01952 203054   Fax: 01952 290628

Staffordshire Ralph Mitchell
Stafford Borough Council, Development Department, Civic Offices, Riverside, Stafford, Staffordshire ST16 3AQ. Tel: 01785 229597   Fax: 01785 619419

Suffolk Rod Blackmore
'Rosemount', Gazeley, Newmarket, Suffolk CB8 8RF   Tel: 01638 750228

Wiltshire Richard Gulliver
4 St Thomas's Square, Salisbury, Wiltshire SP1 1BA   Tel & Fax: 01722 324900

Wiltshire Alan Crouch
4 St. Thomas's Square, Salisbury, Wiltshire SP1 1BA. Tel & Fax: 01722 324900

Note 2
Chapter 1 Membership
The SALTEX Exhibition is held annually at Windsor Racecourse, Windsor, Berkshire. The exhibition is organised by The Institute of Groundsmanship and provides groundsmen/persons involved in managing and working with sporting and amenity facilities. Manufacturers, suppliers of equipment, machinery, materials and services are comprehensively represented. Every day The Institute mount seminars on various aspects of Groundsmanship including 'the preparation of cricket pitches'. For I.O.G. Contact data see ORGANISATIONS.

Note 3
Chapter 2 Fund-raising
Sportsmatch Funding
The Sportsmatch concept has become an excellent form of funding new projects at grass roots level. The scheme was launched in 1992 and during its eleven years over 2700 companies have contributed some £50 million in 72 different sports. Sportsmatch acts as an incentive by offering to double the pot of money available on a £ for £ matching basis. Priority areas for Sportsmatch are schools, young people, disability sport and community sport.

There is now an increased emphasis for improving sporting opportunities for women and girls, ethnic minorities and those in Sports Action Zones (areas of urban and rural deprivation.

Any club or school can apply, for a matching award of £1000 up to £50000, you can have up to 3 sponsors per project, each putting in a minimum of £1000 and the sponsorship can last from one to three years, for any one project. Sponsorship can be in cash or kind. Projects being sponsored should be aiming to increase participation at the grass roots and/or improve skills; they should be new activities or an expansion of existing activities, they should provide links to the community and ensure long-term benefits.

In cricketing terms, Sportsmatch will be used to match the amount put up by a sponsor, who has agreed to sponsor a cricket match. Where the match is raising funds for a specific improvement in club premises/ground that will improve facilities for the disabled, ethnic members who are either currently members or might be future members, of the club.

If your club is considering using Sportsmatch, do not look for your sponsor till you have obtained a link with them, **benefits cannot be retrospective.**

The sponsor should be either new to sports sponsorship or increasing his previous years budget by the said sum. Discuss all the terms with the scheme manager at Sportsmatch. Eighty per cent of applications reviewed by them are approved. From the time of application till acceptance takes a minimum of six weeks.

Note 4
Chapter 2   Fund-raising
To organise Corporate Hospitality

There are a few tried and tested ways of raising money for the club. They all need lots of organising and also good marketing. The club organises a Corporate Hospitality event at their ground, based around a staged cricket match which must include famous sports and TV stars to play against the local team. The main requirement (which will be the core fund raising activity) is a large marquee, furnished with tables & chairs and containing all the necessary equipment for preparing and serving and eating food. A separate annex will be required for the out of sight food preparation.The club then markets each table to local businesses who will in turn expect to be paying for excellent hospitality over their lunch whilst watching the cricket match unfold in front of them. Furthermore these businesses will expect to be given the opportunity of meeting some of the famous names and having them mix with their guests/clients at the table.There will of course be a roped off seating area in front of the marquee reserved for the later stages of the day but still within range of the bar and afternoon tea. Portable toilet facilities will also have to be hired and strategically sited somewhere behind the marquee.

The publicity that is generated within the locality about this forthcoming event allows the club to invite the general public to the ground via an organised and manned entrance to watch the day's play. It is vital to erect some attractive side shows and childrens activities within the ground all of them being income earners. It is also worth trying to get a bar licence for a public bar away from the the marquee and the pavilion which if well manned will produce good income. Next consider printing a decent programme much of which should be financed by advertising. The teams, club performances, history of the club, space for autographs, all have a place in this programme and which should act as an entry ticket and have a number the winner being drawn for a prize at the end of the day.

All we have mentioned must be carefully costed in advance. The more that the club

PLAN Cricket

can squeeze out of local business in the way of sponsorship the better. The club has within its membership a variety of working people who can twist the arm of their employer to give support and the club also deals locally with brewers, who are always looking out for publicity.remember that the more you save in expenses the better the profit.corporate hospitality packages costs should include: The entry ticket, the programme, a special lunch and tea, special seating area, the opportunity to meet the players, a proportion of the Loo hire, a 'free drink' for the principal and his/her guests.

Note 5
Chapter 2 Fund-raising
The Event Programme

How to create the Programme:
Most clubs when organising a special cricket match to raise funds, create a programme, which also doubles as an entrance ticket. This should not cost less than £5, this should not include a charge for the car park. Unless your ground is very accessible by public transport, it is best NOT to charge people to park their cars. You might deter them from attending.

It is worthwhile considering charging a lesser price for sales prior to the event, this guarantees valuable funds whatever the weather and money in advance of the event taking place. Take great care to include somewhere in the programme that 'No money will be returned if the match is not played due to bad weather', this can be placed inside the programme, but it must be printed.

Use the Front Cover to promote the event. Choose carefully the information you are going to place on the front Cover, white space is as important as the words. Keep the message simple.

What event is taking place? When is it being held and where and what time does it start? Are there any special arrangements – Raffles, stalls selling produce – Free Car Park etc., What is the cost of the Programme?

Inside pages can include:

¶ A Foreword by the Club President.

¶ Details of the teams that are playing, if some are County or Test cricketers – carry photographs and statistics. Find journalists or celebrities to write articles on humour, historical features and/or details of why your club wishes to raise the funds. Include data on any specific club 'character'.

¶ Give details on special promotions taking place during the match.

¶ You might like to number the programmes and give the winner a prize.

If you wish to sell advertisements in your programme, remember the printer will charge the club for his work to produce it, the more you are charged the less your profit. Do not charge too much – it is unlikely for the advertiser will gain any reward from his investment. (Never tell any advertiser this fact). When preparing for gaining advertisements, to whom should you sell? Think of all the companies that supply the club (who stands to do well if the club succeeds), remember if you have a good attendance, probably your village shops and garage will also make money.

All the members can ask friendly shops, companies and local promoters to sup-

124

port your programme. Others to include, solicitors, accountants, alcohol companies, ground equipment manufacturers, groundsman's materials and machinery companies and breweries.

Invite a kiosk to sell ices and hotdogs, usually they will give you a percentage of the 'takings', make a contract beforehand.

Another easy way to gain money, is by printing one-liners:
This is for local companies who are prepared to support but who do not wish to have a large outlay: e.g. 'After the match visit Tony's wine bar' and charge them say £20 a line. Print 30 to a page and you have £600.

Have a blank page for autographs, but name it 'Autographs'.

Once you have printed the programme, then arrange that as many as possible **sell** the programme. But keep records who has the responsibility to make sales and record their names, and advise you need any unsold copies to be returned for sales on the match day itself. Make sure all proceeds are supplied to the Treasurer from the sales.

During the match:
Arrange a rota for pairs of club members to look after entrance fees.

Rope off the pavilion sitting area.

Organise your raffle – arrange for the car park to be attended again on a shift basis, at the entrances put up notices to state what are the charges for adults and children and members. Arrange that the stalls and products for sale are in place before the game starts. Arrange for the treasurer or his assistant to have lots of change and that he makes regular calls to 'bank' the returns, this is usually in the boot of his car.

Remember to feed the workers.

One method to guarantee your spectators turn out is to run an under 12/13/14 match (whichever is feasible) say 20 overs match in the morning, prior to the main feature. All the parents/grandparents will come along and watch. BUT make sure they pay to watch the BIG match. Arrange for the winners/losers to be presented with medals to mark the occasion, preferably with a notable doing the presentation.

Ensure all junior players have the opportunity to meet the professional players. Once the match is over make sure all the rubbish is collected and removed. Any signs put up to bring the customers along must be taken down and not left to other days. Also make sure the pavilion is left tidy and clean, for those who are wishing to use it next.

Note 6
Chapter 2 Fund-raising
Special Donations

If your club needs a new pavilion, an extension or a product requiring capital funds and there is a 'peg' on which you can create publicity e.g. A very old club, a very young club, the most young members – famous or infamous reasons, then you work out how much is required and send out begging letters to all famous people you know are keen on cricket, asking them to become a patron, if you receive a donation, write an immediate 'Thank You' letter. Plus letters to MCC, ECB, Your County Cricket Club, Melbourne CC, Commentators (individually by name), the press etc. A club recently raised £90000 by this method. Set up an appeal with a Committee to run it.

Note 7
Chapter 2 Fund-raising
Friends of [your] Cricket Club

This is an ongoing method of fund-raising. All that is required is for a club member to have use of a computer and be methodical and thorough. He/she must send out regular mailings of literature keeping 'The Friends' aware of the club activities. The operator will keep accurate records of addresses, telephone numbers and e-mail data. Each friend normally receives the following items prior to the season:

¶ A newsletter advising about all club activities.
¶ A fixture card.
¶ Details of Memorabilia for Sale
¶ Details of all special events and promotions.

A specially prepared letter from The President or Chairman thanking the person for being a Friend of the club and offering a welcome whenever they wish to visit the club.

¶ Either a club tie or a special 'Friends of [your] club tie'.A charge is made covering all administrative costs, postage, plus the cost of the tie and a nominal profit charge.

Note 8
Chapter 2 Fund-raising
Guy Fawkes Bonfire Night

To organise a public invited/member promoted BONFIRE NIGHT with Fireworks, you do not require a licence. However it is vital that you have responsible persons to organise the event and you take very careful precautions to ensure only specific personnel set the fireworks alight.

It is advisable that your club has a medical resource on site and if possible medically trained officers and doctor available.

You can have stalls to sell hotdogs, hamburgers and soft drinks and make large profits from this method of fundraising, the key is quality organisation and pre-planning. Promote the event well in advance. Have an entrance charge, arrange car parking well away from the place where the event is taking place for safety reasons. Advise and speak with the police. Arrange with 'Highways' for local signposting. Think about the prevailing wind, if possible arrange cover in case of bad weather. TAKE GREAT CARE that all fireworks are kept in a safe environment, have marshals to ensure no unruly behaviour puts the event into a hazardous situation. Check with your insurance that Public Liability is covered. Invite Rotary or similar organisation to support your club and give a portion of the profits to charity, this will encourage external public support.

Note 9
Chapter 2 Fund-raising
Organising The Club Ball

The first requirement is setting up your sub-committee, for this event needs careful planning and demands careful costing, for major expenditure is demanded before a proper return is achieved – the profit can be thousands of pounds.

Many clubs use a marquee which is a costly overhead, add the band and catering and one is talking capital expenditure. Individuals should be asked to bring parties of ten guests or more and make serious commitment.

Planning should start eighteen months in advance.

Opposing teams might agree to bring a part to swell the numbers.

If held in a marquee the club ground can be used as a car park – remember to clearly rope off the square. Use the pavilion for a bar.

Organise toilet facilities for the ladies. Have an auction – plus a raffle.

Buy your wine in bulk, try and make profits on your food. Think about having a breakfast for those who stay late into the night. Marquee decorations are most important.

It is advisable to have an MC to operate the whole evening, plus a team of helpers who operate the wine sales and raffles – the committee will split the various responsibilities and the Treasurer will be very involved.

Note 10
Chapter 2 Fund-raising
A Race Night

For this to be successful, it has to be well planned and executed. It is usually effected throughout an evening and including some seven to eight races. The idea is for each race to be sponsored by a company for a sum of money. Individuals buy a horse for a sum and can name them. Like at a racecourse you bet on the winner, second and third and the race is shown using a projector and screen. If organised well the whole event might be sponsored bringing in even more money. Each race is mounted every 20 minutes and form of the horses can be accessed as on an actual race meeting. The key to its effectiveness is the organisation and how much everyone becomes involved. Winning owners also win the sponsored races amounts.

Note 11
Chapter 2 Fund-raising
A Sponsored Walk or other event

The strength of this type of occasion is that it is possible to gain funds from people outside the club members creating the funds. It is sensible to offer quality prizes for those who either gain the most money or complete the greatest achievements.

Organisation again is the key to success, if we use the term 'walk' as the event, then organising the course is important, so that as many as possible can complete at least one circuit. There are several points at which those competing can gain sustenance, and there are marshals at various points in case of injury. Medical support is at hand for minor injuries. Competitors obtain sponsors and following the event it is vital there is a collecting date for when money has been collected and handed in. Also announce the winners and what was achieved and by whom. The organiser should try and arrange the event to be held throughout a whole day, so those unable to come in the morning can attend in the afternoon. This type of event builds club morale. Often the club brewer will provide a barrel of beer and other company's support by supplying prizes. For those unable to take part, encourage them to make a donation. If the club has a large youth section, then groups should receive encouragement with prizes for various ages.

Note 12
Chapter 2   Fund-raising
Club Ground Painting

Another form of Fundraising that has become popular is having your Club home ground painted by the celebrated artist, Jocelyn Galsworthy.

She has painted most of the leading Test Match grounds around the world. In consequence any club that follows this procedure has both, a wonderful record of the ground and also an investment that increases in value year after year.

The procedure is for the club to contact her and arrange for the painting of the picture. This is either bought by the club or its Chairman/President or Founder. Then, depending on the size of the club, it will be decided how many prints should be made, these will be available framed or unframed, these will be charged by the painter, but it is normal for the club to add on a profit factor. The Club will probably buy extra copies for presentation to various club officers as 'Thank You' presents.

Note 13
Chapter 2   Websites
Website suppliers

¶   www.play-cricket.com
¶   www.hitscricket.com

Note 14
Chapter 3   Club Image
Manufacturers and Suppliers of Club Leisurewear and Training wear

The leading mail order companies all supply competitively priced customised clothing: (All these companies sell a full range of cricket equipment from all the leading manufacturers throughout the year).

A.J.Sports 72 Wimbledon Stadium Business Centre, Rosemary Road, London SW17 0BA Tel: 020 8879 7866

Astoria CSW, Sophia Gardens, Cardiff, CS11 9XR Tel: 02920 409 398

Beckenham Cricket Specialists 181A High Street, Beckenham, Kent BR3 1AE Tel: 020 8663 3582

Bourne Sports Glebe Street, Stoke-on-Trent ST4 1HP Tel: 01782 410411

Fordham Sports 81-85 Robin Hood Way, Kingston Vale, London SW15 3PW Tel: 020 8974 5654

Morrant Group Unit 5, Station Estate, Eastwood Close, South Woodford, London E18 1BY Tel: 0208530 5307

Romida Sports 18 Shaw Road, Newhey, Rochdale, Lancs. OL16 4LT. Tel: 01706 882444

Veekay Sports 31 Bond Street, Ealing, London W5 5AS Tel: 020 8579 3389.

Other companies who provide customised cricket clothing include:

Chase Sports Dummer Down Farm, Dummer, Hants. RG25 2AR Tel: 01256 398666

Duncan Fearnley Cricket Sales Unit 10, Sherriff Street, Worcester WR4 9AB Tel: 01905 612981

Gray-Nicolls (Suppliers of coloured clothing), Station Road, Robertsbridge, East Sussex TN32 5DH Tel: 01580 880357

Gunn & Moore 119/121 Stanstead Road, Forest Hill, London SE23 1HJ Tel: 020 8291 3344

Specialist suppliers of customised clothing are:

Allez (UK), The Old Granary, Floud Lane, West Meon, Nr. Petersfield, Hants. GU32 1JE Tel: 01730 829685

Club Colours The Knitting Mill, Parkside, Fore Hamlet, Ipswich, Suffolk IP3 8AF Tel: 01473 215228

Duke Sportswear Unit 4, Magdalene Road, Torquay TQ1 4AF Tel: 01803 292012

First Impressions (Stac brand), Willow Tree House, 38 Pinewood Grove, New Haw, Surrey KT12 3BU Tel: 0870 744 0172

Fullers Clubwear 26 Waltham Rise, Melton Mowbray, Leics. LE13 1EJ Tel: 01664 566850

Kudos – The Clothing Company 42 Watergate Road, Dewsbury, West Yorkshire WF12 9QB Tel: 01494 713 007

Luke Eyres Unit 7, Henry Crabb Road, Littleport, Cambs. CB6 1SE Tel: 01353 863125

Maddocks & Dick 231 Canongate, The Royal Mile, Edinburgh EH8 8BJ Tel: 0131 556 6012

A. & M. McClellan 94/96 Moorside Road, Swinton, Manchester Tel: 0161 794 1169

James Rawlinson Stonecross Way, March, Cambs. PE15 9DH Tel: 01354 650666

PLAN Cricket

Rochford Sports Knitwear Summerleigh, Quaperlke Street, Bruton, Somerset BA10 0GH Tel: 01749 813240

Signature Sports Leith Vale, Standon Lane, Ockley, Dorking, Surrey website: www.signaturesports.co.uk

Tie Rack Corporate Capital Interchange Way, Brentford, Middx. TW8 0EX Tel: 020 8230 2345

Willow Sportswear (Dept. PC), The Willows, 70 Harden Lane, Wilsden, Bradford BD15 0EU. Tel: 01535 275854

Note 15
Chapter 3 Cricket Equipment
Manufacturers of Cricket Equipment

Bradbury Podshaver's Barn, Pound Lane, Bishop's Lydeard, Somerset TA4 3DW Tel: 01823 430009

Chase Sport Dummer Down Farm, Dummer, Hampshire RG25 2AR Tel: 01256 398666

Crown Bats 42 Watergate Road, Dewsbury, West Yorkshire WF12 9QB Tel: 01924 469396

Crusader Sport & Leisure Main Road, Hallow, Worcester WR2 6LL Tel: 01905 641841

Dukes Unit 5, Station Estate, Eastwood Close, South Woodford, London E18 1BY Tel: 020 8530 5307

Easton Sports 43 Gloucester Road, Croydon, Surrey CR0 2DH Tel: 020 8665 0734

Duncan Fearley Cricket Bat Sales Unit 10, Sherriff Street, Worcester WR4 9AB Tel: 01905 612981

First Test Sports & Leisure Willow Tree House, 38 Pinewood Grove, New Haw, Surrey KT15 3BU Tel: 0870 744 0172 (The Stac brand)

Gray-Nicolls Station Road, Robertsbridge, East Sussex TN32 5DH Tel: 01580 880357

Gunn & Moore 119/121 Stanstead Road, Forest Hill, London SE23 1HJ. Tel: 020 8291 3344

Hunts County Bats Royal Oak Passage, Huntingdon, Cambs. PE18 6EA Tel: 01480 451234

Kookaburra Sport Oakley Hay Industrial Estate, Cnr. Fosse Road and Saxon Way East, Corby, Northants. NN18 9EY Tel: 01536 743337

Millichamp & Hall The Willow Yard, Somerset County Cricket Ground, Taunton, Somerset TA1 1YD. Tel: 01823 327755

Newbery Bats The Chalet, The County Ground, Eaton Road, Hove BN3 3AF. Tel: 01273 775770

Peter Kippax Sports Long Row, Off New Works Road, Low Moor, Bradford BD12 0NF   Tel: 01274 608500

Readersport Unit 25, The Alders, 7 Mile Lane, Mereworth, Kent ME18 5JG Tel: 01622 812230

Salix Cricket Bats Butlers Farm, Horseshoe Lane, Langley, Maidstone, Kent ME17 3RJ   Tel: 01622 863380

Slazenger PO Box 8, Carr Gate, Wakefield, West Yorkshire WF2 0XB Tel: 01924 880000

Tiflex Tiflex House, Liskeard, Cornwall PL14 4NB Tel: 01579 320808

Note 16
Chapter 3 Tours & Touring
Tour Organisers and Sports Travel companies

A   Tour Organisers for The United Kingdom

Shire Sports PO Box 142, Nantwich, Cheshire CW5 8JF Tel: 0870 745 8654 Fax: 0870 7458654 Email: tours@shiresports.co.uk Director: E. Middleton

Good Sports Travel (incorporating Three River Cricket Tours) PO Box 352, Cheltenham DO, Gloucestershire GL54 5ZB Tel: (!01742 882363) 01451 851022 Fax: 01451 851023 Email: sports@goodsportstravel.co.uk Director: M. Edwards

Great Central Sports and Leisure Address: 3 Weaver Drive, Rugby, Warwickshire CV23 9SR Tel: 01788 542441 Email: enquiries@gcleisure.co.uk Director: K. Quinney

Sportsbreak PO Box 246, Northwich, Cheshire CW9 9FJ Tel: 01606 45766 Fax: 01606 331255 Email: sportbreak@amserve.net Director: M. Johns

Titan Groups Inbound Tours Hitours House, Crossoak Lane, Redhill, Surrey RH1 5EX Tel: 01293 450600 Email: ecb@titantravel.co.uk Director: R. Moore

PLAN Cricket

B   Tour Organisers for Europe

Gullivers Sports Travel Fiddington Manor, Tewkesbury, Gloucestershire GL20 7BJ
Tel: 01684 293175 Fax: 01684 297926
Email: gullivers@gulliverspotrs.co.uk Director: J.Davison

Those Tour operators already included covering the United Kingdom are equally capable of organising Tours for European destinations.

Clubs prepared to organise their own tours should visit the ECC website at: www.ecc.cricket.org , or telephone Ian Stuart or Alison Smith on 020 7432 1019 for more information.

Channel Island tours are very popular, all the clubs are most hospitable and welcoming. Contacts are as follows:

Jersey Island CC:

David Taylor – Tel. 01534 759284
Chris Minty – Tel. 01534 745846

Guernsey Island CC:
John Barker – Tel. 01481 723358
Mike Kinder – Tel. 01481 249420

For those clubs wishing to be a little more adventurous, a fairly new destination is Prague; this has many attractions, excellent nightlife, very inexpensive cost of living and excellent shopping.
Contact: Mr Jones – by email: dobroubobr@yahoo.com

C   Long Haul Tour Organisers for the remainder of the world

Clubworld Sports 112 Beckenham Roiad, Beckenham, Kent BR3 4RH Tel: 020 8663 0110/0112
Email: info@clubworldsports.com Director: B. Cantle

The Cricket Tour Company 1 Glenmore, Heath End Road, Great Kingshill HP15 6HS Tel: 01494 713007
Email: info@crictours.com Director: B.Corcoran

Gullivers Sports Travel Fiddington Manor, Tewkesbury, Gloucestershire GL20 7BJ
Tel: 01684 293175 Fax: 01684 297926
Email: gullivers@gulliverspotrs.co.uk Director: J.Davison

Specialist cricket tour organisers throughout the world:

Living with the Lions PO Box 31345, London SW11 1GG
Tel: 020 223 57367/0870 444 0007
Email: info@livingwiththelions.co.uk Directors: M. & P. Arnold

Paragon Sports Management 63 Kew Green, Kew, Surrey TW9 3AH Tel: 020 8332

9009 mobile: 07718535335
Email: mike.martin@paragonsportsmanagement.com Director: M. Martin

Sport Abroad Kuoni House, Dorking, Surrey RH5 4AZ
Tel: 01306 744345 Fax: 01306 744380
Email:info@sportabroad.co.uk Director: T. Davies

The Sporting Traveller The Old Forge, 36b West Street, Reigate,
Surrey RH2 9BX Tel: 01737 244398
Email: sales@thesportingtraveller.com Director: N. Hunt

The ATOL Licence
The Civil Aviation Authority warns all travellers to make sure that their air holiday is booked with a recognised ATOL (Air Travel Organisers' Licensing) holder.
Helen Simpson, director of the Consumer Protection Group at the CAA, says 'ATOL
is the only financial protection scheme for flights and air holidays, booked in the
UK. If an ATOL tour operator fails, your money is safe and you won't be stranded
abroad. You can check if your holiday is protected by looking for the ATOL stamp,
or by visiting the ATOL
website at: www.atol.org.uk

As already noted, when choosing tour operators it is essential that they are suitably bonded, ideally
with ABTA, ATOL and IATA. This ensures that your money is safe.

Note 17
Chapter 3 Training & Coaching
Training & Coaching and Organisations

Association of Cricket Coaches (ACC)
Warwickshire County Cricket Ground, Edgbaston,
Birmingham, West Midlands B5 7QX. Telephone no.: 0121 440 1748
Fax: 0121 446 6344 mobile: 0385 527115
Coach Education Manager: Gordon Lord email: gordon.lord@ecb.co.uk

Association of Cricket Umpires & Scorers (ACU&S)
361 West Barnes Lane, Motspur Park, New Malden, Surrey KT3 6JF
Tel: 020 8336 0586
A General View of the Association Barrie Stuart-King, Chairman
The Association of Cricket Umpires (as it was first named) began modestly in a South London
Pub in 1953, with 24 members concerned not only at the low standard of umpiring but also at
the low esteem in which Umpires were held. Led by the Founder and first General Secretary,
Tom Smith, the Association worked on both the competence of the Umpire and his status. It
was not too long before a parallel need for Scorers became all too apparent and also had to be
tackled. The Association has come a long way since that modest beginning.
From the first, training was paramount. Initially it could be little better than some more
knowledgeable Umpires going through the Laws with the less well informed, discussing how

PLAN Cricket

the written word would become a reality on the field of play.

Now the Association has a Training Board, with an elected Regional Training Officer in each of the twelve United Kingdom Regions. Hundreds of courses are organised locally, during the winter, by Branches and Affiliated Associations.

The Association also holds both residential weekend and one-day Annual Development Forums for Instructors, Examiners and Assessors, supplemented by more local seminars on a less regular basis. Sponsored by Emirates Airlines, the Association produced a video of the sweeping changes that were introduced in the new Laws 2000 Code by the MCC, endorsed by the ECB and the MCC.

Concomitant with major changes in its training programmes, the Association has similarly modernised the administration and structure of its examinations, replacing its written Papers with all-visual-oral formats. This is in preparation for the introduction, in 2005, of a new, ACU&S/ECB jointly administered, National Umpire Grading System, designed to encourage national consistency in both the interpretation and application of the Laws as well as field-craft technique. An Examination Board parallels the Training Board that comprises the elected Regional Examination Officer from each Region. These officers organise and administer all aspects of the Association's multi-level examinations processes throughout their respective Regions, including the arrangements for independent marking and assessments. Currently, the Examination Board has overall responsibility for the conduct of examinations, although, with effect from 2004, this responsibility will devolve onto a new Education & Development Board that will replace the separate Training and Examination Boards. The development and setting of examinations is the responsibility of the Examinations Select Committee working in close collaboration with the ACU&S Technical Committee and responsible to the Education and Development Board.

Sitting alongside – and represented on – the Training and Examination Boards is the Scorers' Board, comprising the 12 Regional Scorer Officers. The Scorers Board is charged with the responsibility for all Scorer instruction in concert with the Regional Training Officers and for setting Scorer Examination papers on behalf of the Examination Board.

In 1994 the Association changed its title to incorporate 'and Scorers', recognition of the increasing involvement of the often unsung members of the 'third team'.

The Association has spread overseas, with members in over forty countries, from Australia to Zimbabwe, via Japan and Switzerland.

Administration, too, has seen changes as radical as those in training and examinations. At first, everything was administered from Headquarters. During the 1970s when the Association's growth made this impossible to continue efficiently, 10 geographic Regions were created and the tasks divided up between them.

With an expanding membership, the volume of administrative work continued to increase to such a level that it was considered necessary to employ a full-time Administration Manager, the first, full-time, paid official in the Association's history. In addition to co-ordinating the paperwork and activities throughout the 12 Regions, the Administration Manager, based in Camberley, is also the initial point of contact for all enquiries from both within and without the Association.

The appointment of a full-time, paid, Administration Manager has released the voluntary Executive Officers to switch from the routine and mundane day-to-day life-blood activities that are an inherent part of a growing organisation to concentrate on crucial aspects of future policy. Through the activities of the Association, the profile and status of the grass-roots Umpire and Scorer, indeed of the Association itself, has improved dramatically since those early years. Now there is An annual grant from the England and Wales Cricket Board (ECB) towards the annual overhead costs of the Association. It is the ECB's insistence that, whenever/wherever possible, only ACU&S Qualified Full Members should officiate in their Recreational Cricket competitions. Have direct representation on the ECB Recreational Cricket Advisory Board; plus direct representation (two members of the Technical Committee) on the MCC Laws Working Party. The previous support by National Grid as a modest collateral to its huge sponsorship of the International Umpires Panel; the £30,000 sponsorship of the ACU&S Laws 2000 Code video by Emirates Airlines in 2000; and a 2-year, £200,000, sponsorship from the Post Office during the years 2001 – 2003, demonstrate how, not only the cricket world at large, but also high-profile commercial organisations, now identify ACU&S as synonymous with umpiring and scoring outside the First Class game.

The Presidents of ACU&S

Throughout the 50 years of its existence – 1953 to 2003 - the Association has had only four Presidents. The first, until his untimely death in June 1958, was Mr Douglas R Jardine.

He was followed by a member of his 1932/33 England Test team to Australia, Sir George Allen CBE, TD, known affectionately by everyone as "Gubby", who, during the 31 years he was President of the Association, became a valued friend, guide and mentor to the Association and its officers. From 1955-1961 he was, simultaneously, also Chairman of the England selectors. Always wearing a Qualified Full Members' tie to official functions, Gubby demonstrated a constant, genuine, interest in the Association's development and activities and was a regular attendee at Annual General Meetings. Gubby, too, died in office on 29th November 1989 aged 87.

Gubby's successor as the Association's President was Sir Colin Cowdrey, CBE, a man who made forty appearances for England. Sir Colin was first capped by Kent CCC in 1951 and went on to captain the County from 1957 to 1971. His Test Career for England spanned the 17 years from 1954 until 1971 during which period he made 11 overseas tours. He played a record 114 times for England, including 23 as Captain, scored 107 centuries, 22 of which he made in Test Matches. At the time, he was also England's leading run scorer and catcher.

After retiring from the First Class game in 1976, Sir Colin maintained an active role in cricket. He was made a Freeman of the City of London in 1962; was a Past President of MCC; and 1993 saw him stand down after an outstanding spell as Chairman of the International Cricket Conference. Sir Colin's services were further recognised in 1997 with a Life Peerage, taking the title of Lord Cowdrey of Tonbridge, CBE. Like his predecessors, Lord Colin Cowdrey died in office, on 5 December 2000, aged 67.

Our current President, The Lord Griffiths of Govilon, MC, is no stranger to cricket or its politics. In 1946, whilst at Cambridge University, and the University's fastest bowler, he opened with Trevor Bailey. On leaving Cambridge he played for Glamorgan and was a member of Wilf Wooller's 1948 County Championship winning side.

Some may know him best as a barrister, judge and subsequently Law Lord, but his other sporting connections are equally impressive. President of the MCC (1990-1991) and Captain of the Royal and Ancient at St Andrews (1993-1994), are but two of his former offices; followed, in recent years, by Chairman of the MCC Laws Review Committee that was responsible for drafting the new Laws 2000 Code. Even more recently, Lord Griffiths has taken on the challenging post of Chairman of the International Cricket Council's Code of Conduct Commission, the body charged with investigating corruption and match-fixing in international cricket. A Vice-President of the Association since 1993, Lord Griffiths is a worthy successor to our three former presidents. He is from a different mould to his predecessors, but will provide influence and representation at the highest levels as befits the Association's international reputation.

British Standards Institute

389 Chiswick High Road, London W4 4AL Tel: 020 8996 9000

Club Cricket Conference

361 West Barnes Lane, Motspur Park, New Malden, Surrey KT3 6JF
Tel: 020 8336 0586   Chief Executive: Barrie Stuart-King

Most recreational cricketers are aware of the Club Cricket Conference (CCC) as a not-for-profit organisation that is owned by its subscribing member clubs, the majority of whom are based in the Home Counties and the South and South-East of England. What is, perhaps, not quite so well known is that, with some 1500 subscribing member clubs; its permanent full-time staff is only four- plus two part-time. Yet the CCC is, by far, the largest of the three Conferences currently serving recreational cricket in England and Wales and the only one fortunate enough to

PLAN Cricket

own outright its own office building,.

Unfortunately, the twin overriding perceptions of the CCC in most people's minds – indeed, amongst most member clubs – are, foremost, of a local full-time Fixture Bureau they call up for help when they are stuck for matches during the season, and secondly an organisation seemingly locked in a time warp with little relevance to, or influence upon, modern recreational cricket.

First, let's correct these mis-perceptions. The full-time Fixtures Bureau facility is only one of a plethora of practical support services and opportunities available to individual member clubs all the year round. These include help with the organisation of custom-tailored, inbound/outbound overseas and domestic cricket tours, and practical assistance - with sources and procurement of playing kit; ground equipment and pavilion security systems at the most advantageous prices through its network of commercial contacts and the member-club database. The CCC also provides a permanent 'Information Help Desk' offering information on best deals in club insurances, with contacts and sources from whom to obtain them; providing help in finding qualified umpires and scorers; giving advice on obtaining visas/work permits for overseas players; locating grounds available for hire; and much more.

The Club Cricket Conference also maintains a Representative XI Squad, whose players are selected from the most outstanding 18-26 year olds nominated by member clubs. The size of the squad has doubled in recent months, following the demise of Under 19 County Board Cricket. The Representative XI plays up to 15 matches a season against such high-profile opponents as MCC, Hampshire CCC Second XI; English Universities, Combined Services, British Police, the League Cricket Conference, the Midlands Club Cricket Conference *et al*, in addition to inbound overseas touring sides such as the Crusaders, Sydney University, the Bradman Foundation, Air India, and Australian Combined Services. Biennially, the Conference selects its strongest Representative side for month-long overseas tours to, in rotation, Australia; West Indies; India, South Africa, and Sri Lanka.

The Future

The National Association of Clubs & League Cricket Conferences (NACLCC)

The NACLCC is a not-for-profit company limited by Guarantee, which has been created by the Club Cricket Conference, the League Cricket Conference and the Midlands Club Cricket Conference as a joint-venture project that will provide a single, independently-funded/sponsored, national body. This working in concert with the England & Wales Cricket Board (ECB), will provide grass-roots support services to - and safeguard and promote the interests of - recreational cricket at all levels throughout the United Kingdom.

The principal Aims and Objects of the NACLCC are to:

¶ help promote, develop, expand and advance the status of recreational clubs; leagues; women's cricket; and cricket for those with disabilities, throughout the United Kingdom;

¶ help promote, improve, develop, and expand the range of support facilities available to recreational clubs, leagues, schools, women's cricket; and cricket for those with disabilities at all levels throughout the United Kingdom;

¶ help promote, encourage and develop greater youth club and community participation in cricket and its associated activities;

¶ help promote, represent, safeguard, develop and generally support the interests of all subscribing NACLCC member Clubs, Leagues, Players, Umpires and Scorers, individually and collectively. It deals with matters of match fixtures, Coach, Umpire and Scorer appointments; domestic and overseas tours; contract negotiations, procurement of kit and equipment; insurances; grant aid applications; sponsorship; groundsmanship; and disciplinary and arbitration proceedings directly related to their cricket activities;

¶ help promote, develop, build upon and maintain existing close collaborative working relationships with the England & Wales Cricket Board (ECB); the Marylebone Cricket Club (MCC); the Association of Cricket Umpires & Scorers (ACU&S); County Cricket Boards; and all other local, regional and national cricket coaching and administrative bodies throughout the United Kingdom, for the betterment of the game generally and the advancement of recreational clubs, leagues, women's cricket and cricket for those with disabilities, in particular.

It is intended that the NACLCC will become reciprocally actively affiliated with both the Association of Cricket Umpires & Scorers (ACU&S) and the National Playing Fields Association (NPFA).The synergy between the NRCC and the ACU&S is self-evident. The ACU&S urgently needs to recruit more, younger, members to train as fully-qualified, graded, competent Umpires and Scorers and its only recruiting ground is from amongst the ranks of recreational club and league cricket/ers. For its part, recreational club and league cricket/ers urgently needs more trained, qualified, competent, Umpires and Scorers!

The project programmes and general activities of the NACLCC will be overseen by a small, professionally-qualified, Executive Management Board. An experienced full-time staff based at the CCC's offices in SE London, will undertake the day-to-day operations.

It is an independent national organisation, with a high-profile national promotion and marketing campaign due to start next year, and with a growing database of subscribing member clubs and leagues throughout the country.

The NACLCC is more attractive to potential sponsors in terms of the reciprocal *quid pro quo's* it can offer, than a regionally-restricted Conference. Similarly, the expansion of *Extra* Cover into a national magazine specifically for recreational club and league cricket, coupled with the annual publication of a national NACLCC Members Reference/Year Book makes them much more attractive to both current and prospective advertisers.

The NACLCC is currently developing - and will be able to offer from next season a much wider and more comprehensive range of support services and activities than either the CCC, or its sister Conferences, operating separately, are currently able to do; eg: expanded Information Help Desk and Fixture Bureau facilities; the provision custom-tailored 'block' insurance policies available exclusively to the NACLCC's collective membership of 3,600 subscribing member clubs; plus, because of its increased 'bulk-purchase' potential, substantial discounts on such items of ground equipment as covers, sight-screens, mowers, scoreboxes/boards etc., and more.

From 2004, both current CCC, LCC and MCCC member clubs, and other clubs and leagues wishing to join the NACLCC will be required to sign up to a Declaration of Acceptance and Endorsement of the NACLCC's terms and conditions of membership that include, for example, commitments to:

¶ embrace a 'family' membership package designed to encourage juniors to join and their supportive dads and mums to train as Coaches (ECB Levels 1-2 Courses) and/or Scorers (ACU&S Introductory Course);

¶ nominate at least one of their members each year to be trained by the ACU&S as a qualified Umpire;

¶ the introduction of annual-rollover recreational player 'contracts' which stipulate a sliding scale of fees that sponsored County or Senior Premier League Clubs who poach, or seek to formally recruit from, or offer a material or financial inducement to leave to, a player from a junior club must pay, by way of compensation for depriving the club of the player's services and for the coaching support and nurturing it has provided to raise him/her to the standard which has attracted the attention of the 'senior' or county club.

England & Wales Cricket Board (ECB)
Lord's Cricket Ground, St John's Wood, London NW8 8QN Tel: 0207 432 1200

PLAN Cricket

European Cricket Council
Lord's Cricket Ground, St. John's Wood, London NW8 8QN

Institute of Groundsmanship (IOG)
19/23 Church Street, Agora, Wolverton, Milton Keynes MK12 5LG
Tel: 01908 312511   Training & Education officer: D.Winn

Institute of Sports Sponsorship – (Sportsmatch)
Francis House, Francis Street, London. SW1P 1DE
Tel: 0207 233 7747 (Sportsmatch) or 0207 828 8771 (See Fundraising Chapter)

International Cricket Council
The Clock Tower, Lord's Cricket Ground, St.John's Wood, London NW8 8QN
Tel: 020 7266 1818

The Lord's Taverners – Cricket's Official Charity
10 Buckingham Gate, London SW1E 6HX
Tel: 020 7821 2828 Fax, 020 7821 2829

The Lord's Taverners started life as a club founded in 1950 by a group of actors who used to enjoy a pint watching the cricket from the old Tavern pub at Lord's. Key early figures were Martin Boddey, the Founder, and fellow actors and friends like John Mills, Jack Hawkins and John Snagge, the sports broadcaster. In the early days, the money raised each year was given to the National Playing Fields Association, whom the Taverners still support, to fund artificial cricket pitches.

Since then The Lord's Taverners has developed into both a Club and a Charity. There are, in total, about 4,000 members. These include The Lady Taverners (founded 1987) as a separate fundraising arm and The Young Lord's Taverners (founded 1988). There are 25 Regional groupings (all volunteer) throughout the UK and Northern Ireland. The Lady Taverners also has 19 Regions.

The Headquarters and small staff is based in London. 80% of the money is raised through events including lunches and dinners, cricket matches and golf days, concerts and quizzes. Since 1950 The Lord's Taverners have given away more than £30 million in grant aid. This is now distributed in the following proportions:

¶ 50% to support youth cricket in the UK, focusing increasingly on the inner city areas
¶ 35% to supplying recreational transport (minibuses) for organisations supporting disabled young people
¶ 15% to supplying sports and recreational equipment for young people with special needs
In 2002 the grant aid amounted to nearly £1.6 million.
The Lord's Taverners continues to draw its members from the world of acting and showbusiness. They also include many sportsmen and women, particularly cricketers, members of the professions and of the world of business and commerce.
The Lord's Taverners is recognised by the England and Wales Cricket Board as the official national charity for recreational cricket.

Clubs and Schools: For details of how to apply for grants, including free cricket equipment bags and grants towards the installation of non turf piches and practice ends, please visit the website – www.lordstaverners,org or telephone: 020 7821 2828.

Marylebone Cricket Club (MCC)
Lord's Ground, St.John's Wood, London NW8 8QN
Tel: 020 7616 8500 or 020 7289 1611   Chief Executive: R.Knight

Founded in 1787, MCC has become the world's most famous cricket club. Today, MCC's role remains as relevant as ever. From guarding the game's Laws to safeguarding its Spirit, and from promoting cricket to young people to looking after Lord's, MCC is committed to the good of the game. The last year has been one of the busiest in MCC history. The Club's teams played almost 500 matches; they undertook numerous overseas tours (to nations as diverse as Fiji and Nepal), to help increase cricket's international appeal; and its women's sides had their busiest season so far. For Lord's, too, it has been a busy year. For example, the ground hosted the last-ever Benson & Heges Cup Final (won by Warwickshire), the brilliant NatWest Series Final (from which India emerged triumphant) and an excellent npower Test (in which Nasser Hussain's England team gained its revenge).Moreover, Lord's staged the second MCC 'Spirit of Cricket Day' last July - part of the Club's worldwide campaign to ensure that a great game is always played in a truly sportsmanlike way. Looking to the future, MCC is investing heavily in Lord's – its home – to ensure that the ground remains world-class, as well as world-famous. For example, the Club is developing three portable pitches on itsNursery Ground, and recently completed a £1.25 million project to remove the main ground's old, clay-based outfield and replace it with a new, faster-draining surface.
Contacting Lord's personnel: MCC can be contacted by e-mail, fax, telephone or post.
   Communications communications@mcc.org.uk via switchboard 020 7286 9545
   Cricket cricket@mcc.org.uk via switchboard 020 7289 9100
   Hospitality hospitality@mcc.org.uk 020 7616 8565 020 7616 8566
   Indoor School indoorschool@mcc.org.uk 020 7616 8612 020 7616 8616
   Laws laws@mcc.org.uk via witchboard, ext. 8512 020 7289 9100
   Lord's Shop lordsshop@mcc.org.uk 020 7616 8570 020 7616 8578
   Lord's Tavern lordstavern@frontpagepubs.com 020 7266 5980 020 7266 5980
   Membership membership@mcc.org.uk 020 7616 8660 020 7616 8666
   Museum museum@mcc.org.uk 020 7616 8656 020 7616 8659
   Ticket Office ticketing@mcc.org.uk 020 7432 1000 020 7616 8700
   Tours of Lord's tours@mcc.org.uk 020 7616 8595 020 7266 3825

National Playing Fields Association
Stanley House, St Chad's Place,London WC1X 9HH Tel: 020 7833 5360

Sport England
(Lottery Funds) – Capital Grants
Hagley Road, Birmingham B16 8TT Tel: 0845 7649649 Or direct: 0121 456 3444

Sports Turf Research Institute
St Ives Research Station, Bingley, West Yorkshire D14 1AV Tel: 01274 565131

Notes 18-20
Chapter 4 External Facilities
Ground Equipment

Ground Equipment Companies

1   Artificial Pitches

Club Surfaces The Barn, Bisham Grange, Nr. Marlow, Bucks. SL7 1RS
Editorial Supplement p.ooo Tel: 01628 485969 Fax: 01628 471944
email: clubsurfaces@tiscali.co.uk Directors: K.McGuinness and D.Underwood.

Exclusive Leisure 28 Cannock Street, Leicester LE4 9HR
Editorial supplement p.98. Tel: 0116 233 2255 Fax: 0116 246 1561
Email: info@exclusiveleisure.co.uk Directors: M.Percy and S.Percy

Flicx UK Walltree House Farm, Steane, Brackley, Northamptonshire NN13 5NS
Tel: 07900 883630 Fax: 01295 810298 *Editorial Supplement* p.101

Nottssport Premier House,18 Mandervell Road, Oadby, Leicester LE2 5LQ
Tel: 0116 272 0222 Fax: 0116 720617 Email: **info@nottssport.com**
Director: S.Patrick *Editorial supplement* p.102

Peak Sports Unit 4, Ford Street, Stockport, Cheshire SK3 0BT
Tel: 0161 480 2502 Email: sales@peaksports.co.uk
Director: R.Cooke *Editorial supplement*: p.104

Verde Sports Cricket Gabbotts Farm Barn, Bury Lane, Withnell, Chorley PR6
8SW Tel: 01254 831666 Fax: 01254 831066 Email: cricket@verdesports.com
Director: P. Dury *Editorial supplement*: p.105

2 Mowers

Allett Mowers Baden Powell Road, Kirkton Industrial Estate, Arbroath DD11 3LS
Tel: 01241 873841 Fax: 01241 877419 Email: roy.allett@allett.co.uk
Director: R.Allett

Dennis Mowers Ashbourne Road, Kirk Langley, Derby DE6 4NJ
Tel: 01332 824777 Fax: 01332 824525
Email: sales@dennisuk.com Director: I. Howerd

3 Pitch Covers and Ground* Covers

3-D Sports The Runnings, Cheltenham, Gloucestershire GL51 9NJ
Tel: 01242 214819 Fax: 01242 222994 Email: sales@3dsports.co.uk

Jetmarine Unit 1, National Trading Estate, Bramhall Moor Lane, Hazel Grove,
Stockport, Cheshire SK7 5AA Tel: 0161 487 1648 Fax: 0161483 7820
Director: P. Sexton

JMS Cricket 'Byeways', East Parade, Steeton, Keighley, West Yorkshire BD20 6RP
Tel: 01535 654520 Fax: 01535 657309 Email: sales@jmscricket.com
Director J.Smith

Pluvius Pitch Covers 27 Robins Grove, Warwick, Warwickshire CV34 6RF
Tel/Fax: 01926 419302 Director: Mrs S. Hirst

SLR Cricket Company 21 Ferndale Drive, Ratby, Leicester LE6 0LH
Tel: 0116 239 5020 Fax: 0116 239 0489 Email: info@slrcricket.co.uk
Director: I. Reeve

Sporty-Co 19 Melton Road, Burton Lazars, Nr. Melton Mowbray, Leicestershire.
LE14 2UR Tel: 01664 562182 Fax: 01664 481701 Email:sportyco@dial.pipex.com
Directors: Mr & Mrs K. West

PLAN Cricket

Stadia Sports International 19/20, Lancaster Way Business Park, Ely, Cambridgeshire CB6 3NW Tel: 01353 668686 Fax: 01353 669444 Email: sales@stadia-sports.co.uk Directors: J.Hoffman, S. Springthorpe

* Stuart Canvas Products Warren Works, Hardwick Grange, Warrington, Cheshire WA1 4RF Tel: 01925 814525 Fax: 01925 831709 Director: D.Kenyon

* Tildenet Hartcliffe Way, Bristol BS3 5RJ Tel: 0117 9669684 Fax: 0117 Email: enquiries@tildenet.co.uk Director: J.Downey

4   Sight Screens

3-D Sports The Runnings, Cheltenham, Gloucestershire GL51 9NJ Tel: 01242 214819 Fax: 01242 222994 Email: sales@3dsports.co.uk

JMS Cricket 'Byeways', East Parade, Steeton, Keighley, West Yorkshire BD20 6RP Tel: 01535 654520 Fax: 01535 657309 Email: sales@jmscricket.com Director J.Smith

Pluvius Pitch Covers 27 Robins Grove, Warwick, Warwickshire CV34 6RF Tel/Fax: 01926 419302 Director: Mrs. S.Hirst

SLR Cricket Company 21 Ferndale Drive, Ratby, Leicester LE6 0LH Tel: 0116 239 5020 Fax: 0116 239 0489 Email: info@slrcricket.co.uk Director: I.Reeve

Sporty-Co 19 Melton Road, Burton Lazars, Nr. Melton Mowbray, Leicestershire. LE14 2UR Tel: 01664 562182 Fax: 01664 481701 Email:sportyco@dial.pipex.com Directors: Mr. & Mrs. K.West

Stadia Sports International 19/20, Lancaster Way Business Park, Ely, Cambridgeshire CB6 3NW Tel: 01353 668686 Fax: 01353 669444 Email: sales@stadia-sports.co.uk Directors: J.Hoffman, S. Springthorpe

Tildenet Hartcliffe Way, Bristol BS3 5RJ Tel: 0117 9669684 Fax: 0117 Email: enquiries@tildenet.co.uk Director: J.Downey

5   Rollers

Autoguide Equipment Stockley Road, Heddington, Nr. Calne, Wiltshire SN11 0PS Tel: 01380 850885 Fax: 01380 850010 Email: websales@autoguide.co.uk

Swillington Rollers 37 Church Lane, Swillington, Leeds, West Yorkshire LS26 8DY   Tel/ Fax: 01132 875318 mobile: 0776 2631297. Director: E.Smith

6   Scarifiers

Allett Mowers Baden Powell Road, Kirkton Industrial Estate, Arbroath DD11 3LS Tel: 01241 873841 Fax: 01241 877419 Email: roy.allett@allett.co.uk Director: R.Allett *(Ed. In 2003 Allett Mowers bought the stock and the rights to use the name RTS, who manufactured aerators and scarifiers.)*

Sisis Equipment (Macclesfield) Hurdsfield, Macclesfield, Cheshire SK10 2LZ
Tel: 01625 503030 Fax: 01625 427426 Email: info@sisis.u-net.com

7   New Catching Aid – SuperCatch Simulator

A revolutionary invention that simulates a batsman at the crease and tests
All close fielders reactions including the wicket-keeper, can be used with
cricket balls, tennis balls or practice balls.

CBC Associates Potwell House, Purbrook Heath Road, Waterlooville,
Hampshire PO7 5SA Tel: 02392 253662 Fax: 02392 269678
Email: cb-gette@tiscali.co.uk Director/inventor: C.Bazalgette

8   Informative Websites on Groundsmanship

Askagroundsman@jmscricket.com
c/o - **JMS Cricket** 'Byeways', East Parade, Steeton, Keighley, West Yorkshire BD20
6RP Tel:01535 654520 Fax: 01535 657309 Email: sales@jmscricket.com
Director J.Smith

*Pitch*care.com
The Technology Centre, Wolverhampton Science Park,Wolverhampton,
West Midlands WV10 9RU Tel: 01902 824392 Fax: 01902 824393
Email: cricketer@pitchcare.com Directors: J.Richards, D.Saltman

Total Turf Solutions 21 Dunnock Lane, Grange Park, Northampton NN4 5DG
Tel: 01604 674368 mobile: 07973 885775
Email: enquiry@totalturfsolutions.co.uk Directors: D.Bates, A.Lewis.

Note 21
Chapter 4   External Facilities

Scoreboards/Boxes/Fascias

3-D Sports The Runnings, Cheltenham, Gloucestershire GL51 9NJ
Tel: 01242 214819 Fax: 01242 222994 Email: sales@3dsports.co.uk

European Timing Systems Oldbury-on-Severn, Bristol BS35 1PL
Tel: 01454 413606   Fax: 01454415139
Email: cksales@europeantiming.co.uk Director: P.Everton

SLR Cricket Company 21 Ferndale Drive, Ratby, Leicester LE6 0LH
Tel: 0116 239 5020 Fax: 0116 239 0489 Email: info@slrcricket.co.uk
Director: I.Reeve

Sporty-Co 19 Melton Road, Burton Lazars, Nr. Melton Mowbray, Leicestershire.
LE14 2UR Tel: 01664 562182 Fax: 01664 481701 Email:sportyco@dial.pipex.com
Directors: Mr. & Mrs. K.West

Stadia Sports International 19/20, Lancaster Way Business Park, Ely,
Cambridgeshire CB6 3NW Tel: 01353 668686 Fax: 01353 669444
Email: sales@stadia-sports.co.uk Directors: J.Hoffman, S. Springthorpe

PLAN Cricket

Note 22
Chapter 5
Health & Safety: References

A list of Codes of Practice applicable to Foods
Institute of Food Science and Technology ISBN 0 905 367 12X £35

Private Water Supplies Regulations 1991
SI 1991 2790 ISBN 0 11 015872 5 The Stationery Office

Private Water Supplies (Scotland) Regulations 1992
ISBN 0 11 023575 4   The Stationery Office

Supply of Machinery (Safety) Regulations 1992
SI No. 1992 3073 ISBN 0 11 025719 7 The Stationery Office

Workplace (Health Safety & Welfare) Regulations 1992
ISBN 0 11 886332 9 The Stationery Office

Food Handlers – Fitness to work
Department of Health £2.50
Department of Health Distribution Centre, PO Box 410, Wetherby LS23 7LN

Water Bye-laws 1989
Available from regional water supply companies.

Health & Safety: Contacts

Chartered Institute of Environmental Health
Chadwick Court, 15 Hatfields, London SE1 8DJ
Tel: 020 7928 6006 Fax: 020 7261 1960

LACOTS (Local Authorities Co-ordinating Body on Food and Trading Standards). PO Box 6, 1A Robert Street, Croydon CR9 1LG
Tel: 020 8688 1996 Fax: 020 8680 1509

Mobile and Outdoor Caterers Association of G.B. (MOCA)
Centre Court, 1301 Stratford Road, Hall Green, Birmingham B28 9AP
Tel: 0121 693 7000 Fax: 0121 693 7100

Royal Environmental Health Institute of Scotland
3 Manor Place, Edinburgh, EH3 7DH Tel: 0131 225 6999

Royal Society of Health
38 St George's Drive, London SW1V 4BH Tel. 0207 630 0121

The Stationery Office
PO Box 276, London SW8 5DT Tel: 0207 873 9090

Department of Health
Department of Health, Room 501A, Skipton House, 80 London Road,
London SE1 6LW Tel: 020 7972 5071

Appendix 1

Magnotherapy: the Editor's personal experience

Just prior to entering the Army I was very fit, starting on a new career, following many of my forbears, half brothers and father, uncles and cousins. I played cricket in the Summer and Rugby in the winter. After eighteen months I had to have a cartilage removed from my left knee,

This was followed first, by the removal of my kneecap (patella) and then during recovery, two further operations repairing ligaments. After a further year of hospital and recovery I had to undergo another operation as my interfascia lata strip (the muscle from my tibia had become disconnected from below the knee). It took three years to return to rugby and four years to play cricket again. The hospital gave me **ten years** of competitive sport. Fifteen years later I cracked my neck, another rugby injury.Forty four years later – I have had a cartilage removed from my right leg some ten years ago and another operation to my left knee (arthroscopy) some three years ago.

I now play cricket and golf. But a year ago, my surgeon told me I had to give up golf, and on the cricket field I was unable to run and very stationary at first slip, with arthritis in both knees and a back ache for ten years. The only way I still played cricket was through having physiotherapy once a week.

Along comes magnotherapy and the Bioflow Reflex to a very sceptical but 'try anything' hopeful… (Incidentally I was starting to have Carpal Tunnel syndrome in my fingers of both hands).

This Summer I have not worn any supports for either knee, (it is the middle of July), I have played 23 competitive cricket matches, and am playing golf again. What is more I can run again. No backache, almost no knee pain, only patches of Carpal Tunnel syndrome. Strained muscles now recover much faster. I have moved away from the slips and close catching positions making everybody much happier. When I first wore the 'Reflex' it took three weeks before I saw any relief and it does not work for everyone. But having 90 days to test, or your money returned, seemed well worthwhile. Now I am trying their other products. I am 65 this year. C.B.

Appendix 2

STOP PRESS Chapter 2 The Law

Change in the Law with regard the Application for a Licence to sell Alcohol in a Cricket Club

Currently, a cricket club requiring a licence, makes an application to a Licensing Magistrate. This will change with effect from early 2005 when the Reform of the Licensing Act 2003 is implemented. If the club already holds a licence then the application will be made to the Licensing Officer of the Council. For clubs requiring a new licence, there will be two requirements: the Club will need a 'Premises' Licence, and the operator of the bar will require a 'Personal' licence; for this they will need to demonstrate some innkeeping knowledge. Submission will be to the Licensing Officer of the Council. If there are objections to the licence by other parties, then the submission will be put through a Licensing Magistrate.

Appendix 3

Setting Goals

Every Club, whether at its formation or those clubs with a long history, should take 'stock' of its aims and activities at regular intervals. Realistically it would be opportune if this was done every time a new President starts his term of office, at the most it should be every five years.

Most Presidential terms are between 2 to 6 years. The larger the Club the shorter should be the period that should elapse before checks are made.

For the club that is starting its life this will be covered separately. For those clubs that are already established – this is for your club. Each senior officer should be constantly looking at how he/she can improve their department and making the club more efficient, so members are able to gain the best enjoyment from its operation. For instance, it is rare for a club to be so financially secure that it does not require extra funding.

Similarly, those clubs that either lease or rent their ground and pavilion (even own it), they all need to plan for, both the maintenance of their ground and its buildings.

All the 'Teams' should set relative 'goals' as to what is attainable. Are coaching and improved training facilities required? Are there either amateur or professional coaches/trainers within the club or do they need to be recruited? Is it enough to let individuals plan their own season – week-by-week preparation? This will differ from club to club and will depend upon standards of play and the ages of players, PLUS and probably of greatest importance, the aspirations of the club and its members.

Does the club play any other sport in the close season? Dependent on facilities, 'other' sports may include – Hockey, Table Tennis and/or an all year round Golf section. Hockey has the great benefit to helping maintain the ground as well as the fitness of members.

If the club has a bar facility, this can also provide healthy bar profits throughout the year. Whatever extra facilities are used there will be benefits for all concerned. But planning and organisation must be incorporated. Events do not just occur. If not properly arranged, then club members and friends lose heart, lose the enjoyment and financially the extra activity will be a drain on finances rather than a benefit.

Extra 'activities' might attract new members, for sportsmen and women will become more interactive, this breeds camararderie and competition.

As people become closer-knit then other periphery activities such as Club Dinners, Tours and touring all gain momentum. Obviously some clubs will not be as competitive or responsible as others.

Many 'wandering' type clubs (not owning or responsible for a ground/pavilion maintenance) play the game for the enjoyment of 'Match' days. They will have lesser targets to set.

Alternatively the County and town clubs have more challenges to maintain, they have responsibilities to their members to maintain, to attain far more, both individually and collectively. Prestige and success in representative appearances will be important. This will include consideration of spectators and their facilities.

But every club has a common responsibility – 'the improvement and support of youth'. Ignore them or limit their involvement at your peril. For they are the 'lifeblood' of every club's tomorrow. Those clubs that invest in youngsters at all standards, the clubs that will succeed and will be seen to flourish.

Once the club Management Committee has been set in place and club officers are elected, then they will have the responsibility to set up the Club rules.

It will be necessary to decide the standard of cricket they wish to play.

They will know whether they are going to lease a ground, hire or rent it or play on Council pitches. It might start out as a 'wandering' club, playing all away matches on other people's grounds. Whilst obtaining a base of their own.

Like the established club it is important to set out 'Aims'.

Every club needs members, it will be necessary to decide how a new player joins the club, will it be through the method of being proposed and seconded by a member, or can they just pay their dues and play. There will need to be a policy for younger cricketers and the management committee will need to establish a member to look after the younger element, deciding what age groups will be accepted. All teams should have a plan of training and being coached, not just before the season, but during the season and in the winter months.

The new Treasurer will need to set up 'his financial year'. Accounts system, where to bank and the necessary administration.

Club officers must decide how players are to be transported, insurance of buildings and personnel, insurance for those preparing food, plus health and safety. If the club has a pavilion, then the question of a licensing facility must be thought about, if this is a factor, then bar items need proper storage and security. As most club houses are somewhat remote and easy prey for thieves.

It is sensible to have an honorary club solicitor to control all the legal requirements. Factors such as:

1. Contracts for those who are on the club's workforce.
2. Property contracts on buildings and machinery.
3. Rates – Grants – Loans – Council plans for the area.
4. Rights of Way, supply of water and electricity. VAT requirements.
5. Handling of boundary disputes with near neighbours.

Appendix 4

Are your Members/Officials CRB cleared?

The Association of Cricket Umpires and Scorers has recently had meetings with The ECB to discuss the safety of their members.

For both Umpires and Scorers may find themselves in the proximity of young persons, either in the changing room or showers without a chaperon. The scorer – either male/female can be in a small scorebox on the other side of the cricket field, totally at risk, should a young person decide to point the finger. Alternatively, the young person is at risk, should there be an adult with them who is tempted to behave improperly.

All cricket Club Administrators now have a responsibility to their members to warn them of the hazards that we have totally innocently never considered. So often a player 'past their prime' will be playing in the 'lower' sides as a coach or manager to give them experience, he must now be aware that when showering he should be either alone or ensure another adult is in attendance.

The ACU & S, are having all their members CRB cleared – (Criminal Records Bureau). Cricket is well behind other sports and those who administer the game should be aware of their responsibilities in ALL cricket clubs. **This is not a subject to be ignored.**

If someone has had a 'past' that includes misbehaviour to a young person, they know they should not be in a position where young people are involved. Has your Club Committee tackled the issue?

'Children have a right to be safe and happy in the sports activities that they, or their parents or carers, choose and parents have a right to believe that the sports clubs or organisations to which they entrust their children are safe. All sports organisations have, therefore, a duty of care for children for whom they provide activities or services. Sometimes, however, there are people who work, or seek to work, in children's sport who may pose a risk to children and who may harm them.' {NSPCC, **sports**check, July 2002}

The England and Wales Cricket Board Limited (ECB) is committed to ensuring that all young people (those under the age of 18 years) who play cricket have a positive experience, and that their safety and welfare is paramount.

The ECB has developed a new policy and procedures which aim to ensure that everyone accepts their responsibility towards the duty of care for young people. **The Welfare of Young People in Cricket Policy** ensures that there are correct and comprehensive reporting procedures, promotion of good practice and sound recruitment procedures for all individuals working within cricket. The ECB recognises that it is not the responsibility of those individuals working in cricket to determine if abuse has taken place but it is their responsibility to act upon and report any concerns.

Who has responsibility for the Welfare of Young People in Cricket?
All adults who have contact with or are responsible for young people in cricket including:

ECB Staff
County Boards – volunteers and staff
Clubs and Leagues
Coaches and Leaders
Team Managers
Umpires and Scorers   Volunteers
Parents

What is the Welfare of Young People in Cricket Policy?
The Welfare of Young People in Cricket Policy is written to support and ensure that all clubs, leagues, County Boards, coaches, umpires and scorers and individuals working within cricket protect young people. The Policy provides guidelines on:

> Good practice when working with young people
> Codes of Conduct
> What to do if there is a concern with regard to a young person or behaviour of an adult towards a young person
> Appropriate recruitment and screening process of volunteers/staff
> How to manage teams away from the club and on overnight tours

How to adopt and implement the **Welfare of Young People in Cricket Policy**

The ECB will have the authority through the policy and procedures to:

¶   Prohibit the involvement of an individual, within cricket, on the basis of conviction, caution or concern by the police or social services
¶   Discipline any individual who is deemed to have breached the relevant codes of conduct or for gross misconduct

The ECB is committed to ensuring that all County Boards, clubs, leagues, Umpire and Scorers Associations and associated cricketing organisations are supported to adopt and implement the policy at a local level. This will be achieved through:

¶   Education and training (see table below)
¶   Guidance notes accompanying the policy
¶   Guidance notes on specific areas, e.g. Self Disclosure/CRB checks
¶   The appointment of County Board Welfare Officers and Club Welfare Officers

Who does the policy apply to?
All adults working with young people in cricket within the following context:

¶   All members of the ECB Coaches Association
¶   All licensed coaches
¶   All members of the Association of Cricket Umpires and Scorers
¶   All affiliated clubs
¶   All clubs working towards or who have achieved Club Mark
¶   All associated cricketing organisations who adopt and work within the ECB Welfare of Young People Policy e.g. Leagues

Education and Training
The ECB is committed to supporting all those working with young people

151

PLAN Cricket

through education and training opportunities in child protection.

The following courses are available.

Training Opportunity	Who should attend
sports coach UK *Good Practice and Child Protection*	Coaches* Team Managers* Adults working with young people paid or voluntary†
ECB *Cricket Specific – Good Practice* *and Child Protection*	Coaches* Team Managers* Adults working with young people paid or voluntary†
ECB Designated Person's Training	County Board Welfare Officers* Club Welfare Officers*
NSPCC Educare	Volunteers/staff with no direct contact with young people†

* ECB requirement
† ECB srongly recommend

For Further information on any of the training opportunities please contact your Cricket Development Officer or the Coach Education Department at Edgbaston

Where can I access the policy?
The Policy is available through www.playcricket.com

The Policy will also be provided as a resource as part of the Designated Person's Training for County Board and Club Welfare Officers.

In compiling a first book of reference for so many activities, there will be a number of omissions and changing factors that have occurred during the writing and production of PLAN Cricket. We would be pleased to receive notice of any changes, additions or comments for future updates.

The Authors

PLAN Cricket

PLAN Cricket

PLAN Cricket

PLAN Cricket: the Administrator's Bible

by Christopher Bazalgette and John Appleyard

ORDER FORM

To Potwell Press, Potwell House,
Purbrook Heath Road, Waterlooville,
Hampshire PO7 5SA

Please send me____ copy/ies of PLAN Cricket
@ £9.99 per copy (post free).

Discount for 10 or more copies 20%
i.e. @ £8.00 per copy (post free).

Cheque enclosed for £   payable to 'Potwell Press'

NAME

ADDRESS

POSTCODE

TELEPHONE NO